Praise for *The Power to Get Things Done*

"What a great book! I _____ ill
cause most readers to _____ o
that!' I love practical ti_____
and this book contains _____
straight in, find somet_____ new habit,
and start making a diffe_____ your life straight away."

— Andy Gilbert, CEO, Go MAD Thinking; bestselling
author of ten books, including *Go MAD - The Art of
Making a Difference* and the *Thinking for Business
Success* podcast series

"Just imagine how much more successful you'd be if you
could always count on being able to motivate yourself to
do whatever you know you should do. *The Power to Get
Things Done* can actually make that happen. Think of it as
extremely practical, user-friendly rocket science! It's filled
with ideas that make sense and really work."

— Chris Crouch, partner, DME Leadership Development
Consulting; author of *Getting Organized* and *Sifting*

"I started reading this book with a sense of smugness.
Having written three books and run my own business for
twenty years, I've always had a penchant for getting
things done—or so I thought. But as I read further, I realized how much I needed this book fifteen years ago! The
authors do more than explain how and why we avoid doing what we should be doing. They provide easy-to-im-
plement step-by-step techniques for overcoming inaction.
In a world where distraction and procrastination are en-
demic, I believe that individuals in any profession who
follow the lessons in this book will be rewarded with a
dramatic increase in productivity and personal accom-
plishment. This is an important and well-written book, so
get your own copy and guard it with your life!"

— Paul du Toit, managing director, Congruence Training
(Pty) Ltd.; author of *You Can Present with Confidence*
and coauthor of *The Exceptional Speaker*

"Finally a book that provides a clear road map for getting things done. This is a must read for every leader."

—Lenora Billings-Harris, coauthor of *TRAILBLAZERS: How Top Business Leaders are Accelerating Results through Inclusion and Diversity* and author of *The Diversity Advantage: A Guide to Making Diversity Work*

"The Power to Get Things Done is an essential and vital handbook for achieving your goals. Chris Cooper and Steve Levinson have created a fantastic toolkit to give business people the edge in today's hyper-competitive marketplace."

—Jeff B. Cohen, Esq., Beverly Hills attorney who as a child played Chunk in the film *The Goonies*; author of *The Dealmaker's Ten Commandments*

"The Power to Get Things Done is a powerful tool for anybody who wants to 'up' their game. It clearly and effectively addresses one of the major obstacles to success both personally and in business: The failure to execute. It describes and dissects how and why, in spite of our best intentions, we are often unable to motivate ourselves to achieve important personal goals or bring projects successfully to completion. It ultimately provides solid, yet simple-to-implement techniques that will give you the power to overcome the forces that are blocking your path to success."

—Mark Larson, vice chairman, Digi-Key Corporation; under Mark's leadership as president, sales increased from $800,000 to $1,760,000,000 and employment grew from 14 to more than 3,500 worldwide

THE
POWER
TO GET THINGS
DONE

(WHETHER YOU FEEL LIKE IT OR NOT)

STEVE LEVINSON, PhD,
AND CHRIS COOPER

A PERIGEE BOOK

PERIGEE
An imprint of Penguin Random House LLC
375 Hudson Street, New York, New York 10014

THE POWER TO GET THINGS DONE

Library of Congress Cataloging-in-Publication Data
Levinson, Steve, author.
The power to get things done : (whether you feel like it or not) /
Steve Levinson, PhD, and Chris Cooper. — First edition.
pages cm
ISBN 978-0-399-17584-8 (pbk.)
1. Intentionalism. 2. Goal (Psychology) 3. Motivation (Psychology)
4. Success—Psychological aspects. I. Title.
BF619.5.L462 2015
158.1—dc23   2015032539

First edition: December 2015

PRINTED IN THE UNITED STATES OF AMERICA

1   3   5   7   9   10   8   6   4   2

Text design by Elke Sigal
All illustrations are original works created exclusively for this book
by cartoonist Huw Aaron, huwaaron.com.

CONTENTS

CONTENTS

FOREWORD

Whether you're in business for yourself or you work for a company, the better able you are to do what you intend to do, whether you feel like it or not, the more successful you're likely to be. Without a doubt, the ability to turn good intentions into action is one of the most valuable assets that anyone who is serious about success can have.

Clearly, however, some of us are naturally better at this than others, and a rare few are even blessed with built-in unstoppable determination; they are veritable productivity machines. For them, there's no space at all between a good intention and the action it calls for. If they decide something should be done, they just do it—whether they feel like it or not.

But what if, like most of us, your determination is anything but unstoppable? What if you're not naturally driven to instantly turn every good intention into action? What if, like most people who want to be successful, you sometimes—maybe even often—

know exactly what you should do but still put off doing it, or do it without the enthusiasm and energy it takes to do it well, or never even get around to doing it at all?

What can we do about this? How do we make ourselves do the things we know we should do but don't feel like doing? Are you simply doomed to settle for less success?

With this book, Levinson and Cooper provide the answers to these questions and more. They explain that just because you may not be a natural-born success machine with built-in, unstoppable determination, it most certainly does *not* mean you have to settle. You *can* improve your ability to turn your good intentions into success-producing action, and no, you don't need a brain transplant, a personality transfusion, or years of therapy. All it takes is knowing *how* to improve by learning and applying a few simple, clever principles, concepts, insights, and strategies.

The premise of *The Power to Get Things Done* is quite exciting when you really think about it. Just imagine what a difference it would make to be able to do the success-producing things you know you should do even when you dread doing them. Whether procrastination is built into your nature or it simply gets the best of you from time to time, no longer will you fall victim to it. No longer will you think yourself into inaction on a project or fall into the rut of doing nothing for fear that what you do won't be perfect.

If you're serious about being successful, you can *make* your own unstoppable determination whenever you need it! If you ask me, there couldn't be a more priceless investment in your own future.

—IVAN MISNER, PhD,
New York Times bestselling author
and founder of BNI

INTRODUCTION

Whether you run your own business or work for someone else, you've probably got a lot on your plate. Unfortunately, much of it may not be all that appetizing. Along with the portion of your work that you truly feel like doing comes a generous helping of things you'd rather not do. Yet to be successful, you obviously can't just do the things you're eager to do. You also have to do the things that you don't feel like doing.

You probably truly *intend* to do most of the unpleasant things that you decide you should do. But do you actually do them? In other words, do you *follow through*?

Really, do you?

You see, how well you follow through matters. It matters a lot. If you're not consistently doing the things you know you should be doing, you're simply working against yourself. Yes, you're in your own way. You're preventing yourself from being as successful as you could be.

How do we know? Steve is a clinical psychologist, inventor, entrepreneur, and CEO who specializes in helping people follow through on their own good intentions. Chris, who describes himself as a "business elevationist," is a business consultant, executive mentor, and coach who draws on extensive executive-level experience in corporations to elevate performance. First as employees and later as business owners, we've walked in your shoes. We learned the hard way just how much it matters to be able to do whatever we intend to do. Until we actually learned how to follow through, we had our share of follow-through failures. And trust us, they were not pretty.

But that's not all. As consultants, we've seen client after client struggle—and often fail—to do the many success-producing things they know they should do but don't feel like doing. And we've seen the amazing things that clients can accomplish once they actually learn how to consistently turn their good intentions into action.

We wrote this book because we're passionate about calling attention to the vital—but, amazingly, largely overlooked—role that follow-through plays in success. And we're frustrated by society's failure to fully recognize just how important and just how teachable follow-through skills are.

The purpose of this book is simple: to teach you how to consistently turn your good intentions into action so you can be as successful as possible in the work you do.

The book is based on these two premises:

1. The better able you are to do what you know you should do, whether you feel like it or not, the more success you can achieve in your business, job, or career.

2. By learning and applying a few simple but powerful follow-through concepts and strategies, you can dramatically improve your ability to follow through.

WHAT TO EXPECT

We're convinced that reading this book will contribute generously to your future success. But be prepared: We might make you a little uncomfortable along the way. That's because we won't be whispering sweet nothings in your ear. We'll challenge some assumptions you may not even be aware of making. We won't hesitate to tell you the truth about how poor follow-through is robbing you of success. And we won't let you pretend that you can do a better job of following through just by trying harder. Instead we'll tell you why you have to stop pretending and start pushing, pulling, prodding, tricking, and forcing yourself into doing—and keeping on doing—the unappealing things you know you must do to be successful.

And, yes, we'll show you how.

HOW TO USE THIS BOOK

We realize that you're busy, which is why we tried to write this book in a way that would allow you to benefit from it regardless of how much time and effort you're willing and able to invest in reading it.

If you have the time and interest, by all means, please read the entire book. The first section, which explains why it's so hard to follow through and why it's so important, will provide you with an important foundation for the practical advice we'll give you later on. The questions at the end of each chapter are designed to further stimulate your thinking about how to turn your own good intentions into action.

If you just can't wait to get down to the nuts and bolts of how to follow through better, you can skip the foundation and start reading at Part Two. You can always come back later and read Part One.

Regardless of how you read this book initially, we hope that you'll revisit it from time to time. We're confident that once you start paying more attention to how you go about turning your good intentions into action, you'll get something new and valuable each time you visit.

THE
POWER
TO GET THINGS
DONE

PART ONE

Why It's So Hard to Follow Through

Perhaps the most valuable result of all education is the ability to make yourself do the thing you have to do when it ought to be done, whether you like it or not. It is the first lesson that ought to be learned and however early a person's training begins, it is probably the last lesson a person learns thoroughly.

—THOMAS HUXLEY

In this section, we'll explain why it's so hard to do the things you know you should do but don't feel like doing. You'll learn why poor follow-through is not exactly your fault and why greater independence can actually bring special follow-through challenges.

CHAPTER 1

WHY MOTIVATION ISN'T ENOUGH

The truth will set you free, but first it will piss you off.

—GLORIA STEINEM

Meet Edward. He started his own technology consulting business a few months ago. He's come to the conclusion that his business will grow at a much faster rate if he starts spending more of his time making sales calls. Edward certainly knows how to make sales calls. In fact, he's pretty good at it. But unfortunately, there's nothing he dislikes doing more. Still, there's not a shred of a doubt in Edward's mind about what he should do. He most definitely should make more sales calls—a lot more. After all, he's got a lot on the line, and he badly wants his business to succeed. So Edward promises himself that from now on he'll make lots of sales calls even though he hates making them.

But will Edward actually make more sales calls?

Will he follow through on his good intention? Even if he starts, will he keep it up, or will he quickly fizzle out? It seems only logical that Edward's strong motivation to succeed will *overrule* his distaste for making sales calls. But will it?

How about Megan? She's a department manager for a large chemical company. She just discovered an opportunity to significantly improve her department's bottom line. All she has to do is begin closely monitoring the department's spending on outside services. She knows exactly what she needs to do, knows how to do it, and can certainly afford to spend the fifteen minutes or less a week it will take. The only problem is that, fifteen minutes or not, Megan can't stand doing the kind of tedious detail work that would be required. Still, because she cares about her department's financial performance and its implications for her career, she promises herself that she will start doing the pesky monitoring anyway.

But will Megan actually do the monitoring? And even if she starts, will she continue? In other words, despite her distaste for the success-producing task she's promised to do, will she consistently do what she intends to do? You'd certainly think so. After all, her intention is an expression of her expertise and good judgment as an executive. It points to a way to satisfy her desire to make her department's performance shine while also increasing the chances that she'll someday be offered a position with greater responsibility, which she definitely wants. So surely her intention should overpower her distaste for doing a simple monitoring job. Surely it should. But will it?

Well, we've known lots of Edwards and Megans. They identify things both large and small that they know they could do to be more successful. They promise themselves they'll do them. But their promises are no match for that awful "I don't wanna do it!" feeling in their gut.

If the Edwards and Megans and everyone else like them didn't care so much about being successful, failing to follow through wouldn't be such a tragedy. But they do care. They care a great deal. And so do you.

Whenever you feel that "I don't wanna do it!" feeling, it urges you to put the work off. Maybe you do the work anyway but so reluctantly and halfheartedly that it hardly pays; or you start doing it but then quit long before the job is done; or you simply don't do it at all. The bottom line is that whenever you let that "I don't wanna do it!" feeling win, you're robbing yourself of potential and telling failure where to find you.

SUCCESS HINGES ON YOUR ABILITY TO FOLLOW THROUGH

There's no way around it. Whether you're striving to achieve success in your business, job, or career, you must be able to do work that you don't feel like doing. Yet even when you know you *could*, believe you *should*, and promise yourself you *will*, there's a good

> Without the ability to follow through, failure is pretty much a sure thing.

chance that you *won't*. That's right, you'll neglect some of the success-producing work you don't feel like doing. Having the ability to follow through doesn't absolutely guarantee success. But without the ability to follow through, failure is pretty much a sure thing.

Like us, you've probably worked hard and dreamed hard to get where you are, and you're probably eager to go further. You really can't afford to neglect things that you know can contribute to your success. So why in the world don't you just do the things you know you should do to be as successful as you genuinely want to be? Why would you ever fail to act in accord with your own good intentions? Why wouldn't you always follow through?

WHY WE DON'T FOLLOW THROUGH

You'll never guess what prevents us from understanding why we don't follow through. It's *logic*. Not enough logic? No! The problem is too much logic! Without even realizing it, we make assumptions that are irresistibly logical but altogether wrong.

In order to understand what makes it so hard to follow through, we have to pay less attention to how we logically think things should work, and pay more attention to how things really do work.

Perhaps the most troublesome assumption we make is that the human mind is properly designed for turning good intentions into action. After all, how could it not be? Well, if you stop assuming and start observing, you'll see that the human mind is, in fact, rather miserably designed for follow-through.

POOR FOLLOW-THROUGH ISN'T EXACTLY YOUR FAULT

Poor follow-through—failing to do what you realize you could do, have concluded you should do, and promised yourself you will do—isn't exactly your fault.

We're serious. Yes, you're off the hook. If you're having trouble doing what you intend to do, you can legitimately blame it on the design of the human mind.

Forget about your business, your job, or your career for a moment. As a human being, you're simply not wired to naturally do things you don't feel like doing even if you truly intend to do them.

As a psychologist, Steve decided years ago to try and make sense of why even the most highly motivated people so often fail to act in accord with their own good intentions. To make a very long story short, he eventually made a startling discovery that explains why we humans do such a lousy job of doing what we intend to do. His discovery led to a theory that made its official debut in 1998 in *Following Through*, a book he wrote with his colleague and good friend Pete Greider.

What he discovered is that poor follow-through is caused primarily by the mixed-up way the normal human mind treats good intentions.

It's pretty simple, really. You see, although we tend to worship the human mind because of its awesome capabilities, the truth is, it doesn't do everything right. In fact, when it comes to enabling us to follow through on our good intentions, the mind is a big disappointment.

> When it comes to enabling us to follow through on our good intentions, the mind is a big disappointment.

We humans obviously have an extraordinary ability to use intelligence to figure out what we must do to get whatever we want and need. We can intelligently decide, for example, to forgo an immediate pleasure or perform an unpleasant task *now* in order to achieve an important benefit later on. That's great. The only problem is, amazingly, our intelligent decisions don't *automatically* drive our behavior. You can figure out what you should do, intelligently decide to do it, promise yourself you'll do it, and still not do it.

That's right, the same impressive mind that's so beautifully equipped to figure out what we could and should do to achieve the success we crave doesn't automatically make us do it. If you really think about it, it's unbelievable! Why would the same mind that has such an awesome capacity for making intelligent decisions not also *make us* do what we intelligently decide to do? Why would we be *allowed* to do things we feel like doing when what we feel like doing violates our intentions?

If this sounds like a recipe for trouble, it is.

It certainly doesn't make sense, but it's still true: Our good intentions simply aren't hardwired to our behavior. They don't naturally drive our behavior even though they logically should. Although they tell us what we should do to achieve success, they don't actually require us to do it. And that's a huge problem because much of what they tell us to do we just don't feel like doing.

Suppose you intelligently decide to spend Thursday afternoon tidying up your desk so you can find things more easily, be more productive, and thereby be more successful. It makes sense, so you promise yourself you'll do it. But your good intention won't actually require you to tidy up your desk. It won't even make you feel like tidying up your desk. In fact, there's a good chance that you may feel strongly like *not* tidying up your desk. You may find the task itself distasteful, or you may feel like doing something else instead, like watching a sporting event on television or wandering around aimlessly on the Internet.

Unfortunately, there's a good chance that what you feel like doing will drive your behavior more than your intention will. In other words, even though your intention is smart, how you feel may have more control over what you do. It makes no difference if what you feel like doing is dumb, shortsighted, and success-opposing rather than success-producing.

Neuroscience expert and author Amy Brann, whose company, Synaptic Potential, bridges the gap between neuroscience and organizations, knows all about the paradoxical way the mind treats good intentions. "Our brains are set up to be very responsive to our internal and external environments," she told us. "Unfortunately this means that we often do not follow through with our intentions and need to utilize additional strategies to do the things that are important to us," she explained. "To an extent, we are reward-seeking beings and we are wired for immediate gratification. The trick is to work with, rather than against this."

HOW WE EXPECT MOTIVATION TO WORK

How we think motivation should work is not, in fact, the way it does work.

If motivation worked the way most of us think it should, people like us who strive for success would always do what we intend to do. After all, aren't we highly motivated? Aren't we serious about making our dreams come true? Shouldn't our motivation take us all the way to the finish line? Why would we ever fail to follow through?

Isn't it only logical that if we really want to succeed, we should be able to overcome just about any obstacle? Surely we should be able to make ourselves do unpleasant work if we believe that doing it might contribute, even in a small way, to our success. Shouldn't we automatically feel motivated to do each and every thing that we know will help us be successful?

Yes, it's logical to assume that if we truly want to be successful, and we know that doing a particular success-producing thing will help us succeed, we'll just do it. In fact, it's so logical that we continue to believe it despite the overwhelming evidence that it's just not true!

DON'T BE FOOLED BY OUTLIERS

By the way, logic isn't the only thing that fools us into believing that wanting to succeed should make us do what we intend to do. There are also the stories we hear about truly inspiring people who manage to overcome extraordinary adversity. They keep doing incredibly difficult and unpleasant things day after day, year after year, until they achieve unbelievable success. Their unstoppable drive to succeed seems to offer proof that people—other people—can do what they intend to do when they just put their minds to it.

Don't be fooled. These people are *outliers*. They are rare individuals who seem to be—and may actually be—*wired* differently than the rest of us. They may have been born with different wiring, or they may have had life experiences that rewired them. But whatever made it happen, they now have superhuman determination that allows them—in some cases, compels them—to achieve what the rest of us can only dream of achieving. To be sure, they deserve our awe, admiration, and, yes, our envy. But because they're wired so differently, they are most definitely not us, and they can't really teach us *how* to follow through.

You can do yourself a great disservice by comparing yourself to these extraordinary achievement machines. Do you conclude that you're physically handicapped if you're unable to twist yourself into a pretzel the way a circus contortionist can? Of course not! It's the contortionist who's *abnormal*, not you. And if you have trouble doing what you intend to do, trust us, you're the normal one.

HOW MOTIVATION REALLY DOES WORK

The truth is, wanting to succeed won't automatically make you do the specific success-producing things you don't feel like doing.

Let's break it down further.

- Wanting to succeed won't make you *feel like* doing success-producing things you don't feel like doing. For example, if you conclude that having a clean desk will contribute to your success, but you don't feel like cleaning your desk, you won't feel like cleaning your desk no matter how much you want to succeed.
- What wanting to succeed will do, however, is make you produce good intentions. It will make you promise yourself that you'll clean your desk.
- But here's the problem: Promising yourself that you'll clean your desk won't necessarily make you clean your desk! Your good intention won't automatically have enough power behind it to overcome the resistance to doing something you don't feel like doing.
- You'll clean your desk only if you're sufficiently motivated to overcome the resistance you feel to cleaning your desk. Being motivated to succeed won't do the trick. You have to be motivated *specifically* to clean your desk. For example, if someone were to threaten to shoot you right

now "unless you clean your desk," you'd probably have enough motivation to overcome your resistance.

WELCOME TO REALITY

We know that much of what we're saying may fly in the face of what you've always believed. And we realize it's not easy to suddenly stop believing that wanting to succeed will make you do the particular things you know you must do to succeed. But learning how to follow through starts with facing the truth about why we so often fail to do what we intend to do.

So, welcome to reality, where being motivated to succeed doesn't automatically make you motivated to do the crap you have to do to succeed; where wanting to succeed doesn't put enough power behind your good intentions to overcome the resistance to doing things you don't feel like doing; where the smartest and best good intention is, on its own, no match for a strong feeling in your gut that shouts, "I don't wanna do it!"

IS IT HOPELESS?

So if you don't have the unique brain wiring that makes following through automatic for the lucky outliers we spoke about earlier, are you sunk? Will you have to settle for doing a lousy job of following through? Absolutely not! You can still follow through like a champion.

You just have to learn how to do it. You won't be able to do it the same way that someone who's lucky enough to be wired for follow-through does it. You'll have to do it *manually* rather than automatically. But what matters is that you will be able to do whatever you intend to do and enjoy all the benefits.

The first step is setting aside the false assumptions and wishful thinking that prevent you from moving forward. In the next chapter, we'll help you take that step by taking a fresh, up-close and personal look at the work you intend to do but don't feel like doing.

PUTTING IT INTO PRACTICE

1. What are some of the things you've intended to do but haven't yet done?

2. What are you putting off that's really important?

3. How much is it *costing* you to not do the important things you intend to do?

4. What are some of the things you could accomplish if you had the ability to do whatever you intend to do?

NOTES

_____
_____
_____
_____
_____
_____
_____
_____
_____
_____
_____
_____
_____
_____
_____
_____
_____
_____
_____
_____
_____
_____
_____
_____
_____
_____
_____
_____

CHAPTER 2

UGH! THE WORK YOU DON'T FEEL LIKE DOING

Nothing is so fatiguing as the eternal hanging on
of an uncompleted task.

—WILLIAM JAMES

Think about the things on your work plate that you truly intend to do but don't feel like doing. These are the actions, tasks, and projects that are like unpaved and muddy sections of the road to success. To get to success, you need to get through the mud. But the mud resists your good intentions and threatens to turn the promises you make to yourself into broken promises. Yes, the risk of neglecting the things you don't feel like doing is very real indeed. And it poses a very serious threat to your success.

Andrew can tell you all about it.

When he was a child, Andrew loved to draw.

Now, at the age of thirty-seven, he still loves to draw. In fact, he earns his living by drawing. Andrew is a commercial artist, and a very good one at that. However, the business that Andrew built around his passion and talent for drawing—a business that's the realization of his childhood dream—isn't doing very well. That's because along with the drawing he loves to do, Andrew now has lots of things on his work plate that he doesn't feel at all like doing. And even though he knows that doing those things would contribute to his success, he neglects them.

Andrew hates, for example, preparing price quotations for his customers. He doesn't like having to estimate how much time a project will take him because he doesn't really know for sure and doesn't want to guess and be wrong. The unknowns and risks of getting it wrong drive him crazy. Just thinking about preparing a quote is enough to make Andrew feel sick. And when he feels sick, Andrew often does things that only make matters worse, like going on the Internet, where he wastes hours looking for various things he knows he doesn't need.

Andrew has a great deal invested—both financially and emotionally—in his business being successful. Because he's painfully aware that he has to get these quotations done whether he feels like it or not, he keeps promising himself that "from now on" he'll submit quotations promptly. But he hardly ever does it.

Andrew has plenty of insight. He realizes that he's avoiding work that must be done. He understands why he's avoiding it and why he has to stop. He's looked to friends, family, colleagues, and even a consultant for help. Although he's managed to collect lots of encouragement, a few scoldings, and a practical suggestion or two, the problem persists.

Andrew's inability to do what he doesn't feel like doing does more than just hurt his business. It's beginning to erode his confidence and his morale. It's threatening to turn his childhood dream into an adult nightmare.

Andrew is not only troubled by his failure to do what he intends to do, he's baffled by it. It doesn't make any sense to him. He figures his strong desire to succeed should allow him to overcome his reluctance to do something he'd rather not do. In other words, he assumes that his good intention will have enough oomph to push him through his reluctance.

To Andrew, this assumption is so utterly reasonable that he can't let go of it despite the fact that his actual experience keeps telling him it's wrong.

WHAT'S ON YOUR WORK PLATE?

On your work plate are all the things you know you must do to be as successful as possible. Like Andrew, you have two distinct piles of demands.

In one pile are the demands that represent things you know you should do and also feel like doing. These include the things you dreamed about doing before you started your business, chose your career, or took a job that you were excited to get. They include your passions, the things that excite you, and all the things that come easily or flow naturally for you without stirring up any reluctance, resistance, or avoidance. For Andrew, it was drawing. Drawing for him was like gliding effortlessly down a silky smooth road. Andrew just naturally felt like drawing.

Of course, if the only kind of demands on your work plate were the kind that required you to do things you naturally feel like doing, following through wouldn't be a problem. We rarely have trouble doing the things we naturally feel like doing.

But there are very few people on this planet who are lucky enough to have their work plate filled solely with demands that require them to do what they naturally feel like doing. Even the most talented professional violinist, for example, who's filled with passion for playing that instrument, probably has to practice sometimes when he or she doesn't feel like it.

So unless you're one of the luckiest people in the world, you have a second pile of demands on your work plate. These demands require you to do things you simply don't feel like doing. Some require you to do things you find boring, tedious, or burdensome. Some require you to do things that are just unsatisfying enough to repel and push you away. Some require you to do things that make you feel sick and anxious the way Andrew felt about preparing quotes. Some may require you to do things that are so dreadful that you don't even dare think about doing them.

Yes, this is the pile of demands you wish would go away and leave you alone. Just tell yourself to do what one of these demands requires and a little voice in your head will scream, "I don't wanna do it!"

You tell yourself, "I really should work on that financial report today," and a little voice in your head replies, "I don't wanna do it!"

Surely you've heard the shouts and groans. "Ugh!" "Not that!" "Go away!" "God help me!" "Shoot me!" We've certainly heard them. In fact, we hear them all the time.

There's obviously a huge difference between a demand that requires you to do what you naturally feel like doing and one that requires you to do what you don't feel like doing. It's like the difference between, on the one hand, picking up an adorable puppy with its tail wildly wagging and its tongue licking your face and, on the other hand, picking up a pile of smelly dirty diapers. Although they may weigh the same and the actual amount of physical work required may be the same, the experience is certainly very different. Lifting the puppy feels like it hardly takes any effort at all. There's no real resistance. The puppy wants to be lifted. Not so the pile of dirty diapers. The pile might as well be shouting, "Don't come near me!" It resists. It repels. It makes you want to hold your nose and run the other way. It makes you want to shout, "I don't wanna do it!"

GIVING IT A PROPER NAME

Rob, a seasoned middle manager for a U.S. manufacturing company, heard the voice in his head shout, "I don't wanna do it!" so often that he decided to give a proper name to the demands on his own work plate that require him to do things he doesn't feel like doing. He calls them "goo."

Goo is unpleasant. It's heavy. It's sticky. And it resists and repels. Boy, does it resist and repel!

Rob loves his job. Well, that's only *partly* true. Rob loves only part of his job. It's the part that he actually feels like doing. For Rob, that's the part that involves creative thinking and problem-solving.

When he started his job years ago, Rob wishfully assumed that it would consist entirely of creative thinking and problem-solving. He thought that what he loves doing would completely fill his work plate.

Well, it didn't take long for Rob to discover that there was going to be a second pile of demands on his work plate—a pile that would keep growing and growing and growing and eventually dwarf the first pile. But there it is. It's a towering pile of demands that require him to do things he doesn't feel at all like doing. This is Rob's *goo*.

To say that Rob detests the goo on his work plate would be an understatement. "It totally sucks," he told us. Yet because Rob knows he can't be successful without "doing the goo," he never hesitates to promise himself that he'll do it.

But promising to do it isn't the same as actually doing it. Rob struggles all the time to try to do the things on his work plate that he doesn't feel like doing. Much of it he puts off for "as long as possible." Some of it he puts off for even longer than possible, and he suffers the consequences. Some he starts but then sets aside because, as Rob puts it, "I can only take so much goo without going stark raving mad."

"The goo's got me!"

GOO IS PERSONAL

Everyone we've ever worked with and everyone we've ever known has had plenty of goo on their work plate. Let there be no mistake about it, it's perfectly normal and natural to not feel like doing some, or many, or even most of the things you know you must do to be successful.

There's nothing unusual or unhealthy about having your whole being wince whenever you try to do— or even try to think about doing—things you don't

> It's perfectly normal and natural to not feel like doing some, or many, or even most of the things you know you must do to be successful.

feel like doing. And in our opinion, anyone who tries to tell you otherwise is doing you a great disservice.

Like beauty, goo is in the eyes of the beholder. It's 100 percent personal. What repels you may not repel someone else, and what repels someone else may not repel you. The same task that you'd do nearly anything to avoid might be welcomed by someone else as a gift.

Case in point: When Steve was a health care executive, he had an awesome administrative assistant who he used to jokingly introduce to others as "Maggie—she does my job." Hundreds if not thousands of times during the many years they worked together, Steve would apologetically give Maggie a task or project that he perceived as being tedious and boring enough to induce nausea, vomiting, and possibly suicidal thoughts. What never ceased to amaze him was that the very same hideous task or project that he presented with his eyes rolling would make Maggie's eyes sparkle. What was goo to Steve was nectar from Heaven to Maggie.

Whenever Steve could spend his time dealing with creative big-picture matters, he felt like he was on that same silky smooth road that Andrew was on when he was drawing. He loved dealing with the forest. He didn't care that much for the trees. And, frankly, he felt nothing but contempt for the leaves. But Maggie welcomed the leaves with open arms. In fact, she loved the leaves.

Our point is, it doesn't really matter why a particular action, task, or project triggers that "I don't wanna do it!" feeling for you. It doesn't matter if it makes no sense at all. All that matters is that if it feels like goo to you, it is goo. And if it's goo, you're at risk of neglecting it. And if you do neglect it, you're shooting yourself in the foot—or worse.

Goo is obviously subjective. It doesn't matter how little effort, objectively speaking, something you don't feel like doing requires. All that matters is how much it makes you groan.

Like us, you might feel reluctant to do certain things that, objectively speaking, require such a small amount of effort that it's downright embarrassing. If so, we can assure you that you're in good company. Even the most ambitious people you can imagine often fail to put forth the tiny amount of effort it would take to accomplish something they consider important.

This used to happen to Steve often. While working, he would tell himself, "I really should take a second to put this folder where it belongs right now because if I do, it'll save time and effort and spare me frustration the next time I need it." He was genuinely eager to bring order and convenience to his work environment, and this was one way he knew he could do it. How could anything be easier?

Yet, amazingly, Steve almost always violated his own good intention. It just felt like too much trouble to actually take a second to stand up, open a drawer, and put the file where it belonged. Too much trouble? How in the world could that be? Again, objectively, the amount of effort required was miniscule. But somehow, subjectively, it was enough to defeat a good intention that was intelligently designed to improve the quality of his work life and indirectly contribute to his future success.

Yes, it just doesn't make sense that Steve would avoid putting forth so little effort to achieve a desired result. But does it really matter that it doesn't make sense? What does matter is that, for whatever reason, the miniscule amount of effort required was just too much for him.

Now, you can certainly accuse Steve or anyone else, including yourself, of being just plain *lazy*. But *lazy* just doesn't stick. If you ask people who know Steve, for example, they'll tell you that he's an especially hardworking person. Press them, and they'll back that up with evidence. They'll point to many things he's done that required an enormous amount of sustained effort.

Lazy? We don't think so. Yet somehow Steve was unable—not just once, but time and time and time again—to put forth the fraction of an iota of effort required to keep his office better organized. He confesses that it's still a mystery to him. But he's learned that *not knowing why* is a poor excuse for pretending that it isn't so.

So, again, if it feels like goo to you, it's goo. It doesn't matter if it seems like it should be easy. If it's goo, it's goo. And remember, if it's goo, you might neglect it. And if you do neglect it, you're depriving yourself of success.

AVOIDING GOO IS HARD WORK

Remember Rob? Rob will tell you that whether he's trying to do the goo or is busy avoiding the goo, the goo makes his job miserable.

You see, when Rob said that goo "sucks," he wasn't kidding. Goo literally sucks energy out of you. Avoiding unpleasant work is itself hard work! Although it obviously doesn't accomplish a thing, it does use up energy that you could otherwise use for success-producing activities. So avoiding goo is wasted work. You *pay* for it but you get nothing in return. It's like paying a rental fee for an office you never use. It depletes your resources without giving you any benefit at all.

Wait, it gets even worse. If you're avoiding things you know you should do, you can only scold yourself so many times before your self-confidence and self-esteem start to suffer. This can set off a vicious spiraling of toxic emotions that can actually make you avoid even more, punish yourself even more, and waste even more of the energy and hope you need to be successful.

AN EXTRA HELPING OF GOO FOR EMPLOYEES

If you're an employee, there may be an extra helping of especially repelling goo on your work plate. This is goo that your employer put there. It's made up of demands that not only require you to do things you don't feel like doing, they require you to do things you perceive as being unreasonable, unnecessary, or even at odds with the very purpose of your job. This goo is *stupid goo*!

Now, before we alienate employers, we should make it clear that even those demands that you experience as being the dumbest and most infuriating may be legitimately important and necessary from your employer's point of view. But legitimate or not, it's how you perceive these demands that matters. Yes, if it's stupid goo to you, it's stupid goo.

It can be maddening when your employer requires you to devote time and effort to actions, tasks, and projects that you experience as interfering with your ability to do your job.

Craig, a frustrated department manager for large manufacturing company, complained bitterly to Steve about the "stupid" demands his employer put on his work plate. We believe he spoke for many employees when he insisted, "I can't do my *job* because my *damned job* keeps getting in the way!"

What Craig was conveying is that the stupid goo his employer kept putting on Craig's work plate prevented him from energetically and enthusiastically pursuing the real purpose and substance of his job.

Now, remember, it doesn't matter whether Craig's complaints and the complaints of every other employee who feels the same way are valid or not. What matters is that there's definitely stupid goo on their work plates, and that sets the stage for a drama that, at the very least, wastes lots and lots of energy. The drama features a clash between, on the one hand, an unusually intense desire to avoid doing dumb, wasteful, and unpleasant things and, on the other hand, the realization that their employer may be more likely to punish them for neglecting their *damned job* than for neglecting the *job* they assumed they were there to do!

In addition to our work with clients, we've both had firsthand experience being overwhelmed by employer-initiated stupid goo.

For Chris, it happened when he worked for a snack food business and was responsible for buying the key ingredients for fifteen factories. Due to a reduction in administrative resources, he was forced to enter into a very complex IT system detailed information for every buy he made. He loved doing the deals, but he hated the IT system, which he felt robbed him of valuable time and sanity. So, when another company offered Chris a position he believed would be less *gooey*, he jumped at the opportunity.

For Steve, it happened when the small mission-focused health care organization he worked for was swallowed up by a much larger organization with, shall we say, "different priorities." He watched in horror as the stupid goo on his work plate grew exponentially. (Picture a scene from a bad science fiction film!) The "stupid" things he was required to do took more and more of his time and energy away from things that he believed really mattered and that he loved to do. Pissed off, drained, and unsatisfied, he eventually threw in the towel. After thirty-five satisfying years and a long list of successes that he had gladly worked hard to achieve, stupid goo did Steve in.

Fortunately, Steve did manage to learn some valuable lessons about stupid goo before he quit. He learned, for example, that it takes far less effort to fill out a simple two-page form than it takes to fill out the very same form that you think of as "that stupid, unnecessary, waste-of-time #$@%!!! form." The former is just work. The latter kicks and screams and fusses whenever you get near it.

So even if you're convinced that you deserve a promotion, a salary increase, and a medal for having way smarter priorities than your employer, unless you're ready to throw in the towel, it's worth learning how to get through the stupid goo. Until you do, like all goo, it will suck energy out of you and pose a threat to your success.

PUTTING IT INTO PRACTICE

1. What are the most important tasks or projects you need to get done?

2. Which ones are you already neglecting or at risk of neglecting?

3. Which ones are you actively avoiding?

4. Which ones do you start but quit before you're done?

5. Which ones do you do but with so little enthusiasm that the results may suffer?

NOTES

_____

_____

_____

_____

_____

_____

_____

_____

_____

_____

_____

_____

CHAPTER 3

SPECIAL FOLLOW-THROUGH CHALLENGES FOR BUSINESS OWNERS

By failing to prepare, you are preparing to fail.

—BENJAMIN FRANKLIN

Although this chapter is primarily for business owners, there are three reasons why we urge you to read it even if you don't currently own your own business.

First, you may already be thinking about the possibility of someday running your own business, but even if you aren't, you never know what the future will bring. At the very least, learning now about the special follow-through challenges that business owners face will ensure that if you do find yourself thinking about taking the plunge, you won't overlook an extremely important aspect of the self-employment experience.

Second, if you already enjoy a high degree of independence in your job, or you're striving for a position that offers even greater independence, there's a good chance that you're facing, or someday will face, some of the same follow-through challenges that business owners face every day.

And lastly and perhaps most importantly, this chapter might change the way you think about being an employee. More specifically, you may come to appreciate that some of the very same things you don't like about being an employee actually help you do what you intend to do.

THE HIGHER THE STAKES, THE MORE FOLLOW-THROUGH MATTERS

We're sure that you've gotten the message by now: To be successful, you have to be able to do success-producing things whether you feel like it or not. So if you're serious about being successful, it makes good sense to invest in your ability to follow through.

> Unless you get really good at doing what you intend to do, you're asking for trouble.

If you run your own business, the ability to do what you intend to do matters even more. Because the stakes are so high and the follow-through challenges are so great, investing in your follow-through ability isn't just a good idea, it's a necessity. Unless you get really good at doing what you intend to do, you're asking for trouble.

FREEDOM IS A DOUBLE-EDGED SWORD

A desire for greater freedom probably had a lot to do with your decision to run your own business. Before you set out on your own, you may have spent years as an employee daydreaming about someday having the freedom to fashion your own vision, set your own pace and schedule, choose your own style, and most importantly, decide on your own priorities. Whether it was an easy decision or one you agonized over, you eventually made the decision. You took the plunge. You're free now.

Ah, freedom! What more could you ask for?

Well, in case you haven't noticed, freedom is a double-edged sword. Sure, with the *ceiling* removed, the sky's now the limit on what you can accomplish, and that can be truly exhilarating. But the *floor* is also gone. Yes, you're *free* to fail like you've never failed before. And if you think about it—and maybe you try not to—that can be awfully frightening.

You've put a lot on the line. There's a good chance you've invested some money in your dream, and you've undoubtedly invested lots of time and effort. But there's even more than that at stake. If your business fails, your self-esteem and your reputation could take massive hits. You could end up feeling responsible for dashing your family's hopes for a better life.

You could end up spending years feeling embarrassed, guilty, and demoralized.

Needless to say, you have a lot to lose. What's more, statistically speaking, losing is a real possibility.

You're probably already well aware of the odds that a small business will fail. But just in case you're not, it's time for a reality check. Studies on both sides of the Atlantic indicate that more than half of new businesses will fail within their first four or five years. Yikes! That means that a failure is not just possible; technically speaking, it's more likely than not. With more than twenty-five million small businesses in the United States and United Kingdom combined, it's disturbing to think about just how many dreams will turn into nightmares. You certainly don't want your dream to be one of them.

Unfortunately, there's not much you can do to protect yourself from many of the threats a small business faces. These threats include unwelcome developments in the economy, competition, unforeseen changes in consumer habits and preferences, and sudden technological advances that can, through no fault of your own, destroy your business.

The fact that you can't control many of the threats that can harm your business means that you have to be especially diligent about controlling the threats that you can.

And the biggest of the controllable threats you face may be a threat that many business owners overlook until it's too late. It's the threat of neglecting to do the many success-producing things you know you should do but don't feel like doing. It's the threat of failing by failing to follow through.

We've been in your shoes. We know how intoxicating it can be to finally have the freedom to achieve great things by virtue of your own vision, abilities, and hard work. But it should also be sobering to recognize just how much your success hinges on your ability to do what you intend to do.

Yes, your follow-through ability really does matter. Unless you're consistently able to do the many success-producing things you don't feel like doing, you're placing your business in danger.

We're not exaggerating when we say that follow-through failures can literally kill your business.

And although having your business fail for any reason would stink, failing by failing to do what you intend to do is an especially painful way to end a dream.

> Follow-through failures can literally kill your business.

YOU DON'T KNOW WHAT YOU'VE GOT TILL IT'S GONE

If we've managed to convince you that it's especially important for you as a business owner to be able to do the things you know you should do whether you feel like it or not, get ready for some bad news. Not only is doing what you intend to do more important for peo-

"If only I had learned how
to follow through."

ple who run their own business, unfortunately it's
also a lot harder!

Why? Well, to put it crudely, assuming that you
were an employee before you set out on your own, you
went from being on a short leash to not being on a
leash at all. Yes, now that you own and run your own
business, you're free to do as you please. That may
sound like a good thing, but there's a downside to being free to do as you please. The downside is that
there's a good chance that doing what you please—
doing what you feel like doing—will often be at odds
with what you should be doing and what you intend
to do to make your business prosper.

If you open your eyes wide and look back to when
you were an employee, you'll see that forces in your
work environment pushed you to do the things you
didn't feel like doing. Just think about the expectations
of your superiors, the deadlines, the performance eval-
uations, the competition, the tangible and intangible

rewards and punishments, and all the signs that Big Brother was watching. This was your follow-through infrastructure. It was a largely invisible array of mostly unwelcome forces—some subtle, some not so subtle— that conspired to keep you on track in doing the many things you didn't feel like doing.

Yes, as an employee, you could pretty much count on being prompted, prodded, pressured, pushed, and sometimes even forced to do particular things you knew you had to do but didn't feel like doing.

Beth knows all about being pushed through the goo. She finally wrote a brief report that she had intended to write weeks earlier but kept putting off because she didn't feel like doing it. She had already promised herself at least half a dozen times that she'd do it "tomorrow," but she kept breaking her promises despite the fact that she believed the report would contribute favorably to her future with the company she worked for. The push came in the form of a memo from her supervisor, Rachel, who said that she needed the report by noon on Thursday so she could include it in a presentation she was scheduled to give to upper management.

Without the push from her supervisor, Beth's intention simply didn't have enough horsepower to push her through the resistance she felt to doing what she didn't feel like doing. The memo made her feel like she no longer had a choice. She had to do it. She had to write the &%$#@ report. With the push, she made it through the goo. Beth didn't much like the pressure, but without it, her good intention wasn't taking her to the finish line.

WITHOUT PRESSURE, IT'S EASY TO LET THINGS SLIDE

As an employee, you probably didn't care much for the pressure, either, but guess what? It probably worked. It probably helped you do what you intended to do. Your follow-through infrastructure made it possible—usually not fun, but possible—for you to get some awfully unpleasant work done. It made getting the work done *feel necessary*.

Now, let's be clear about what we mean by "feel necessary." We don't mean the same thing as "thinking it's a good idea" or "believing or knowing it's a smart thing to do." We're referring to an unmistakably urgent, anxious feeling in your gut that says, "I'd better do it or else!"

So think about it. Now that you're on your own and all that nasty pressure is gone, have you noticed how much easier it is to let unpleasant things slide?

As much as you may appreciate no longer feeling accountable to anyone but yourself, without a robust follow-through infrastructure, you're bound to have follow-through problems. Sure, it may feel like a blessing to be free of the pressure you felt as an employee, but when it comes to doing what you intend to do, it's also a curse to not have enough pressure to push you to do the things you just don't feel like doing.

Now that you're on your own, what can you depend on to prompt, prod, pressure, push, and force you to do the many unappealing things you know you have to do make your business succeed? What replaced the pressure you felt as an employee to get through the goo? What can you depend on to make it feel necessary to do the particular success-producing things you intend to do but don't feel like doing?

You may be tempted to answer that having so much at stake and desperately wanting your business to succeed is enough. If so, you're only fooling yourself. Although we're certainly not questioning how motivated you are to succeed, we know that being motivated to succeed isn't the same as feeling like it's necessary to do a particular unpleasant success-producing task that's staring you right in the face. You can only get the task done when you *feel* like—not just know—that you must.

Unless you can get a good push whenever you need it, you won't make it through the goo. Yet as a business owner, there's no ready-made follow-through infrastructure to give you a push whenever you need one. There's no follow-through help of the sort you could count on when you were an employee.

Yes, the funny thing about a follow-through infrastructure is that it rarely looks or feels like help until it's gone.

YOU DON'T KNOW WHAT YOU CAN'T DO UNTIL YOU CAN'T DO IT

A family we know moved to a warmer climate several years ago. Although the house they bought was equipped with a modern electric furnace, they figured they'd never really need it. But last winter, when the temperature dropped to record lows, the furnace didn't work. When they investigated, they discovered that it was no wonder the furnace didn't work. The electrician had neglected to finish wiring it! Until they needed heat, they had no reason to question whether the furnace would be ready and able to produce it.

So it goes with the ability to do what you intend to do. *You never know what you can't do until you can't do it!* When you were an employee and didn't have to rely primarily on your own follow-through ability, how would you have known that your follow-through ability wouldn't be up to the challenges you'd face as a business owner? If you weren't aware of the follow-through infrastructure that invisibly bolstered your ability to do what you intended to do as an employee, you would have had no reason to think you'd have trouble doing what you intended to do as a business owner. In other words, you may have been fooled into thinking that your follow-through ability was better than it really was.

When you set out on your own, you probably discovered some demands on your work plate that you hadn't had to deal with as an employee. Even though these demands required you to do work that was essential to your business's success, you'd had no idea just how much you'd feel like avoiding the particular work they required you to do. Yes, it's going to take an especially powerful push to get through this goo! But wait. Where's the kind of follow-through infrastructure you could depend on as an employee to do the pushing?

Oops. Sounds like you're in store for a rude awakening.

NOT WHAT THEY EXPECTED

Jim, Jennifer, and Dave didn't get what they expected when they made the transition from high-performing employees to business owners. Their high hopes were dashed by follow-through challenges they didn't anticipate and follow-through skills they assumed they had but didn't.

Jim had been a stellar sales representative for a specialty software company. He loved selling, and he couldn't wait to be on his own so he could benefit more fully from his remarkable knack for persuading others to buy.

When Jim was an employee, he was keenly aware of his skills, but he wasn't very aware of all the things his employer did to set the stage for Jim's skills to result in success. For example, he benefited from his employer's excellent lead-generation system. Of course, intellectually, Jim realized that when he was on his own, he'd have to generate his own leads, but he had no idea how much of a problem he'd have getting himself to do it.

Jim realized that his success hinged on his ability to do the whole job well—not just the part he did when he was an employee. He certainly knew how to generate leads, but unlike selling, which he *felt* like doing, Jim sure didn't feel much like generating leads. In fact, he hated it. As a result, he put it off for as long as he could, and when he finally did it, he did it grudgingly, and as he acknowledged, "It shows."

Jim was still a great salesperson. But now that his success depended on his ability to do something that he didn't feel like doing, his talent as a salesperson wasn't producing much success at all. That's because there was nothing to force him to do what he knew he should do. So instead of being a super salesperson on the road to extraordinary success, Jim was afraid he might be a has-been who was on the road to destroying his own business.

Jennifer was a spectacular public relations professional who worked for a large public relations firm. She distinguished herself by responding with remarkable ease, thoroughness, and speed to the many demands of her many clients. She was always incredibly busy—so busy, in fact, that when she announced that she would be leaving to start her own consulting business, her boss gasped, "Oh my God, Jen, I'll have to hire three people to replace you!"

Jennifer had a rude awakening when she started

her own business. Instead of being the ball of fire she had been accustomed to being, she found that most days the fire was out before she got to the second item on her to-do list.

Jennifer struggled to make sense of what had happened to her. As an employee with a steady stream of client demands coming her way, she had consistently been super productive. But now that she was on her own and the sky was the limit, instead of flying higher, which is what she had expected to be doing, she wasn't even getting off the ground.

Jennifer's self-esteem took a nosedive, which only made things worse. Before long, her business was in serious trouble.

So what happened to Jennifer? Like so many others who strike out on their own, she had never really appreciated that her stellar performance as an employee was thanks in part to having a job that allowed her to focus on doing work that she almost always felt like doing. Now that she was on her own, to generate business for herself she had to focus on work she knew she had to do but didn't feel like doing.

As an employee, Jennifer never had to find work because work always found her. So when she daydreamed about how wonderful things would be when she was finally on her own with the freedom to do public relations work the way she chose to do it, it frankly never even occurred to her that she wouldn't feel much like *finding* public relations work.

Dave was a fantastic automobile mechanic who

ran circles around the other mechanics at the bustling auto dealership that employed him. Aware of his own talent and fed up with feeling that his employer was benefiting more from Dave's abilities than Dave was, he decided to open his own repair shop.

Dave was wildly enthusiastic about his new venture. He accomplished a great deal in a relatively short time. He secured a loan, found a good location, invested in equipment, hired a few employees, learned about many of the rules his business would have to comply with, and set up a proper website and an advertising program. It was smooth sailing.

But shortly after he settled into the day-in, day-out nitty-gritty of running his business, Dave's enthusiasm began to fade.

Although it was Dave's extraordinary skill as a mechanic and his passion for fixing cars that had prompted him to start his own business, he soon discovered that he felt neither skillful nor passionate about most of the tasks that filled—or rather *should have* filled—his day as a business owner. In place of the work he loved was work he barely tolerated and sometimes even hated— all the annoying stuff he didn't have to deal with when he was just an employee fixing cars.

Dave started putting off things he knew he needed to do. And he spent more of his time doing the few things he didn't mind doing, like playing endlessly with the company website and looking for the best price on a bigger photocopy machine that he knew he didn't need and couldn't afford.

Dave tried giving himself pep talks and beating himself up, but nothing worked—or at least not for very long. He was getting discouraged and disillusioned. His dream was turning into a nightmare.

THAT WAS THEN, AND THIS IS NOW

Before he was on his own, Jim had a very supportive boss who lavished praise on him all the time. But, as a business owner, without the benefit of a built-in cheering section, Jim struggled, and often failed, to do what he intended to do.

Jennifer had a micromanaging boss who often drove her crazy with his very exacting expectations. But, as a business owner, without someone hovering over her, Jennifer struggled, and often failed, to follow through.

Dave had a demanding and unreasonable boss who tolerated no excuses—including legitimate ones. But, as a business owner, without having to worry about incurring a boss's wrath, Dave struggled, and often failed, to follow through.

As employees, Jim, Jennifer, and Dave didn't recognize the follow-through help they were getting. But when the help was gone, they sure noticed how much harder it was to do what they intended to do.

Again, it's not their fault. As employees, they fantasized about someday having an unfettered opportunity to do and profit from doing the things they loved doing. They thought little, if at all, about all the new goo that would be on their work plate as business owners. They had no way of knowing that when it came time to get through that goo, they'd struggle and maybe fail; that when the rubber hit the road and they had to rely on their own follow-through skills, those skills would not be up to the challenge. They just assumed that their good intentions would have enough horsepower to push them through any and all of the unpleasant work their own business would require them to do. They were wrong.

CHRIS'S CHALLENGING TRANSITION

Back in the 1970s, folk singer Joni Mitchell wrote and performed a popular song called "Big Yellow Taxi" that made the point that we don't always know what we have until we no longer have it. She may as well have been describing Chris's challenging transition from being a corporate executive to running his own business.

As he made his escape from the corporate world, all Chris could think about was that he was finally bidding good riddance to a job that was preventing him from being all he knew he could be. He had no idea that he was also saying good-bye to an invisible but powerful set of props—a follow-through infrastructure—that helped him do the things he knew he had to do even when he didn't feel like doing them.

Back in the early 1990s, Chris was a top-performing salesperson who had won a prestigious sales award.

Chris recalls that there had been enormous team pressure to perform. He still remembers those nerve-racking monthly performance targets and tough meetings where he had to put his performance stats on display.

When he started his own business, Chris was truly excited to be free of all the pressure he'd felt as an employee. However, it didn't take long before he was feeling more anxiety than relief.

Without a telesales team or any real structure for bringing in leads or holding him accountable for digging deep and performing up to his potential, he really struggled. Chris wondered why his business wasn't taking off the way he had thought it would.

Of course, there really wasn't any reason to wonder. Why *would* his business take off? Clearly, he wasn't doing enough to make it take off. It wasn't because he didn't know what to do. He knew exactly what to do. And it wasn't because he didn't promise himself he'd do it. He promised himself time and time again. And it wasn't because he didn't care enough about succeeding. Chris most certainly did care. He cared a great deal.

Chris was disappointed in himself. He was frustrated. And mostly, he was puzzled. He kept asking himself how he could have done so well working for others and now be doing so poorly working for himself. It didn't make any sense to him.

Luckily, Chris came across Steve Levinson and Pete Greider's work on following through (more on this later). Suddenly, things started to make sense to him. He realized that the very same set of forces and circumstances he had regarded as the enemy when he was an employee had also been his friend. He came to appreciate that what he had regarded as only holding him back had also been responsible for propping him up. Chris discovered that without all the pressure—

> It takes enough of the right kind of pressure to get through the goo.

the deadlines, the threats, the expectations, the punishments and rewards—it really was much harder to do what he intended to do.

Fortunately, Chris learned this lesson in time to save his business. He learned that it takes enough of the right kind of pressure to get through the goo. And once he learned how to create his own *friendly* pressure, his business started to prosper just the way he had always hoped it would.

THE INDEPENDENCE YOU WANT CAN BRING FOLLOW-THROUGH CHALLENGES YOU DON'T

If you're employed, don't think you're immune to the kind of rude awakening that small business owners commonly experience after taking the plunge.

You can have a rude awakening whenever you make a transition to a job that allows you to exercise greater independence. That's because having more autonomy also means having less of a follow-through infrastructure to help push you through each of the important things on your work plate that you don't feel like doing. So at the same time you find yourself under more pressure than ever before to achieve big *bottom line* results, you're likely to feel less pressure than you've ever felt before to do each of the specific things you must do in order to achieve the results you want. And without the latter kind of pressure, you're bound to face the same kind of follow-through challenges that business owners face.

> Having more autonomy also means having less of a follow-through infrastructure.

Just ask Anish.

A computer technician who worked in the IT department of a midsize accounting firm, Anish had a reputation for responding quickly and effectively to urgent cries for help from the accounting staff. Besides having a knack for diagnosing and solving all kinds of computer problems, Anish, unlike many of his peers, was really good at giving simple, useful answers to the questions the firm's computer users asked.

Anish had a great reputation. In fact, he was so appreciated that staff members who needed help typically bypassed the proper channels and went directly to Anish for help. He never said no, which, of course, made him far busier than his peers, and that did make things stressful for him at times. Still, because he felt so good about being so appreciated, Anish kept hopping. In fact, he was rather proud of his office nickname, "the Rabbit." Anish was a star and everyone knew it. So when a supervisory position opened up and he expressed interest, it was no surprise to anyone that he was immediately offered the job. Anish eagerly accepted the promotion, which came with a substantial pay raise. Also, because he had faced the same types of problems every day for years, his work was no longer stretching his abilities, and he thought it would be good to face a new set of challenges. He was especially excited about finally having a chance to implement ideas he had been thinking about for years for improving the efficiency and effectiveness of his department's support services.

Although he started his new job with high expectations, before long, Anish's enthusiasm took a nosedive. No longer was the Rabbit happily hopping around the building solving problems for grateful staff members. Instead, a much less energetic Anish spent hours every day more or less waiting and hoping for something to react to. He knew it was now up to him to initiate projects. He had no shortage of ideas. He started working on some, but never really finished any. He spent much of his time just hoping that someone—anyone, please— would call him for help so he could *respond*.

When his job consisted primarily of responding to the routine demands that others placed on him, Anish was a follow-through star. But now that his job consisted primarily of creating demands for himself, it was a totally different story. Anish the Rabbit had turned into Anish the Sloth.

Anish's trademark ability to respond, which had so generously nourished his pride, was no longer visible. In its place was an obvious inability to respond to the demands he now had to create for himself. This eventually undermined his confidence and satisfaction. Anish knew he was headed for serious trouble. He was right. In less than a year, demoralized, he quit his job and left the company rather than suffer the embarrassment of taking a step down the success ladder to a position with less responsibility.

Anish has since thought a lot about what happened to him. He's still not sure whether it was a mistake for him to take the promotion. What he does now know for sure, however, is that it was a mistake—and a whopper at that—for him to take a promotion without anticipating and being prepared to meet the follow-through challenges he was bound to face.

In Part Two of this book, you'll learn about a critical shift in thinking that could have prevented Anish from experiencing a whole lot of pain.

PUTTING IT INTO PRACTICE

1. If you were an employee before you owned your own business, what kind of *follow-through help* did you get from others?

2. Now that you're self-employed, what's replaced that help or what could replace it?

NOTES

_____

_____

_____

_____

_____

_____

_____

_____

_____

_____

_____

_____

_____

_____

_____

_____

PART TWO

From Trying Harder to Trying Smarter

> It ain't what you don't know that gets you
> into trouble. It's what you know for sure
> that just ain't so.
>
> —MARK TWAIN

In this section, we'll first show you how to think about and treat your intentions in a way that maximizes their effectiveness. Then we'll introduce you to the key concepts, principles, and insights that make it possible to create powerful strategies that will transform your good intentions into success-producing action.

Much of what you'll learn in this section draws heavily on the pioneering work that Steve Levinson and Pete Greider did in the 1990s. Their book, Following Through, _still sends a powerful message to individuals, organizations, and society:_ Following through is not about trying harder. It's about trying smarter.

CHAPTER 4

MAKING THE SHIFT

If the wind will not serve, take to the oars.

—LATIN PROVERB

Our goal in this chapter is to help you make a critical shift in your thinking about how to transform your good intentions into action. Once you've made this important shift, you'll think about doing what you intend to do as a predictable result of a very deliberate *manual* process.

So that's the thinking that you'll be shifting *to*. But what about the thinking you're shifting *from*? Please let us set the stage for you to discover the answer.

Take your time in answering this question: *Describe the concrete steps you commonly take to maximize your chances of doing what you intend to do.*

Drawing a blank? We're not surprised. If you do what most people do, you simply cross your fingers and hope for the best.

HOW YOU TRY TO FOLLOW THROUGH

Although you certainly don't think of them as steps or methods per se, without realizing it you may actually be doing some things to try to improve your follow-through.

For example, you probably use the ever-popular but rarely effective *Try Harder* method. If you fail to do what you intend to do, you simply promise yourself that you'll *try harder* next time.

On the surface, this method makes a certain amount of sense. If you're not doing what you intend to do, shouldn't trying harder do the trick? But what exactly does it mean—if it means anything at all—to try harder? Seriously, in concrete terms, what do you do differently when you *try harder*?

Now, if you were to say, "I didn't like where I ended up last time when I made a left turn at this intersection, so next time, I'll turn right," that would be a different story. You'd be making a concrete change in your behavior. Because you'd be doing something different, you'd have a chance to get a different result. But *trying harder*? If you're not doing something different, why would you expect to get a different result?

So when you promise to try harder, are you really promising anything at all?

There are some popular variations of the *Try Harder* method of trying to turbocharge your good intentions. Perhaps you've tried them. (We certainly have.) There's the *Beat Yourself Up and Then Try Harder* method. And there's the *Rah! Rah! and Then Try Harder* method. But even if your own scoldings and/or pep talks result in slight improvements in follow-through, any gains are likely to fade quickly.

MOTIVATION BY INSPIRATION

Another way we try to improve follow-through is by getting inspired. In fact, if you just look around, you'll see that *Motivation by Inspiration* is a widely endorsed and extensively promoted method for motivating ourselves to get difficult things done. One could even argue that it's society's favorite method.

On the one hand, getting inspired can produce truly impressive bursts of follow-through. On the other hand, there's a good reason why you shouldn't rely on inspiration to make your good intentions effective. It isn't reliable! Not only can't you count on inspiration being available when you need it, inspiration-produced motivation is decidedly short-lived. It evaporates quickly.

For example, we hear about a mother who saved her child's life by using her bare hands to lift a heavy car that pinned the child underneath. The story reminds us that we all have awesome, largely untapped potential; that if we just focus intensely enough on our goals, and if we just want badly enough to succeed, we can do amazing things that seem nearly impossible. We feel inspired. With renewed enthusiasm, optimism, and energy, we're sure we can now tackle that important project we've been putting off. Heck, we can do anything!

How long will it take before that intensely satisfying and empowering inspiration-produced motivation fades away and leaves us flat? It usually doesn't take long at all.

Although inspiration can produce a welcome burst of extreme motivation, it's not a sustainable source of power for your good intentions. Do you think the mother who lifted a car off her child could spend eight hours a day lifting cars? Inspiration-fueled motivation can certainly give your good intentions a healthy push. But you can't count on it to keep on pushing.

"I don't get it—I wallpapered my office with inspirational posters, yet I'm still failing."

DON'T LET YOUR GOOD INTENTIONS GET STRANDED

There's another problem with *Motivation by Inspiration*, and it's a problem that's often overlooked. Inspiration-produced motivation is misleading. Despite its short half-life, it can feel convincingly permanent. It can fool you into believing that you'll always have enough follow-through power to do whatever it takes to reach the stars. Frankly, that can be dangerous. In the same way that mistakenly believing that you have plenty of money can cause you to make financial commitments you won't be able to fulfill, mistakenly feeling like you have plenty of follow-through power can cause you to make promises—including big ones—that you simply won't be able to keep.

Let's face it, we want to be inspired. We enjoy it. We like to feel enthusiastic and optimistic. So it's no wonder that we welcome and even actively seek out experiences that will inspire us to reach higher and make us feel like we can do it. We read inspiring books and articles, listen to CDs, and attend workshops, seminars, and speeches. Oh, how we love to get psyched up! In fact, we love it so much, we usually don't notice that it doesn't last nearly as long or work nearly as well as we think it will.

If you've ever been to a conference or training event and come back really pumped up to take action, you know exactly what we're talking about. Remember how excited you were? But then what happened? Where did all that enthusiasm go? What happened to the promises you made to yourself to put those great ideas you learned into practice?

Inspiration, enthusiasm, optimism, a positive attitude—they all have value. Unfortunately, they are too undependable to serve as a primary source of power for your good intentions. Emotions that make you feel "I Can Do It!" are like favorable gusts of wind.

> If you really want to reach *success*, you can't depend on the *wind*. You have to learn how to *row*.

Whenever they're available, you can and should use them to push your good intentions through the goo. But it's a big mistake to rely on them. That's because your good intentions will get stranded if the wind dies down. And, yes, the wind will definitely die down. If you really want to reach *success*, you can't depend on the *wind*. You have to learn how to *row*.

WE'RE NOT ANTI-INSPIRATION— WE'RE PRO-FOLLOW-THROUGH

Okay, we realize that we may have been raining on your parade. We hope you don't think we're just cynical observers of human nature—anti-inspiration, anti-enthusiasm, anti-optimism, anti–positive attitude stick-in-the-muds. We're not. We're just passionately *pro*-follow-through! We don't believe that getting enthusiastic is the secret of success. We believe that the secret of success is knowing how to make yourself do things when you don't feel enthusiastic about doing them.

So go ahead and get inspired whenever you can.

Seek it out, eat it up, and enjoy it. Let it help you do great things. But please, please, please don't depend on it to make your good intentions effective. Trust us, it will not get you through all the goo you have on your work plate. To follow through consistently, you need to be able to deliver power to your intentions whenever they need them.

ARE YOU READY TO MAKE THE SHIFT?

Let's return to the critical shift in thinking we told you about at the beginning of this chapter.

Are you ready to accept that you won't automatically be motivated to do the things you know you must do to turn your dreams into reality? Are you ready to stop relying on inspiration, enthusiasm, optimism, or a positive attitude to drive you to do all the "I don't wanna do it!" things you know you should do day in, day out to achieve success? Are you ready to stop thinking about doing what you intend to do as something that just happens if you're lucky—that is, when the *wind* just happens to blow in your favor? Are you ready to start thinking about turning your good intentions into action as something you deliberately make happen? Are you ready to start thinking about actually doing what you intend to do as *the predictable result of a deliberate manual process*?

In the chapters that follow, we'll tell you all about that deliberate manual process. We'll show you how you can manufacture your own follow-through power whenever you need it. We'll teach you how to give your intentions as much power as they need to overcome as much resistance as you feel.

As you prepare to learn about the nuts and bolts of how to do whatever you intend to do, you might be wondering why you weren't taught how until now. Shouldn't you have learned this long ago? Why didn't you? Heck, why didn't everyone?

The best explanation that we've been able to come up with is that society, amazingly, hasn't yet figured out that follow-through skills are teachable. But they are. And even though it's unfortunate that you weren't taught them long, long ago, it's better late than never.

HOW MUCH WILL YOU INVEST?

If you want to position yourself for success, we can't imagine making a wiser investment than an investment in learning how to follow through. Having the ability to do whatever you intend to do, whether you feel like it or not, will have a huge impact on your business, your job, or your career. Just imagine being able to take whatever you already know—and anything you learn in the future—and transform it with speed and power into success-producing action. Imagine earning a well-deserved reputation for being able to dig into the most unpleasant of tasks and projects and stick with them until the job is done.

Learning how to follow through is like learning most other skills. How much time and effort you're willing and able to invest in lessons and practice will obviously have a bearing on how proficient you'll become. Will you choose to make a small investment and settle for a modest reduction in follow-through failures? Or will you invest whatever it takes to become a bona fide follow-through master? Will your investment be confined to reading this book once and applying whatever *sticks*? Or will you make a point of practicing what you learn and revisiting the book as often as it takes to achieve and maintain the level of proficiency you're after? It's your decision.

THE BENEFITS OF BEING A FOLLOW-THROUGH MASTER

If you do decide to become a follow-through master, we can assure you that you'll reap rewards that go well beyond eliminating the costly consequences of neglecting things you don't feel like doing. You'll stay more focused, be less susceptible to distractions, and be more productive. You'll be able to benefit more from all your other skills, talents, knowledge, experience, and effort.

Follow-through masters always place their intentions in the driver's seat. What they decide they should do, they do. Whatever they decide is important gets their attention, their time, their talent, and their effort. Because their intentions rule, follow-through masters can concentrate on doing the things they believe will make the biggest positive difference.

Being intention-driven makes follow-through masters less susceptible to the kind of forces that so often hijack others' attention and waste their time and energy.

As you've probably noticed, the things that matter most to the success of your business, job, or career are not always what get your attention. What gets your attention is the *squeaky wheels*—the stuff that's right in your face, or that's naturally interesting, or the wheels that are easy and immediately rewarding to grease. Meanwhile we often neglect the quiet wheels. These include all the unsexy tasks that don't demand our attention even though they may hold the key to our success. Follow-through masters pay attention to the important wheels that don't squeak.

> Follow-through masters pay attention to the important wheels that don't squeak.

Before Chris developed his follow-through skills, he was at the mercy of squeaky wheels that represented opportunities to do what he especially enjoyed doing. The problem was, what he enjoyed doing was quite at odds with what he knew he had to do to grow his business.

For example, Chris spent lots of time with social media, which was easy and fun for him. Yet even though he knew that his social media efforts would be largely wasted unless he first got really clear about his goals, objectives, and strategies, "getting clear" was neither easy nor fun for him, so he just kept *playing*. He spent an inordinate amount of time writing newsletters and creating products, which he thoroughly enjoyed doing, while neglecting to do the less enjoyable thing he knew would help him grow his business, which was to gather prospects by calling members of his network.

Because Chris's intentions weren't in the driver's seat, he could easily be lured off track. He jumped at any chance to do what he liked doing instead of what he knew he should be doing. All in all, he wasted lots of time doing ineffective things he felt like doing while neglecting to do the effective things he knew he should do but didn't feel much like doing.

Once he learned how to do whatever he intended to do, Chris was able to stay focused on making his business grow. Because he was no longer so easily distracted by the same squeaky wheels that had previously been getting the lion's share of his *grease*, his business really started to prosper.

WALK, NOT WOBBLE

Follow-through masters enjoy another advantage. Once they decide what they should do, they do it without hesitation.

When Chris reflects on the many super-achievers he's interviewed for his radio show, he's struck by something that the most successful seem to have in common. They adopt crystal-clear intentions and then promptly—we mean promptly—turn them into success-producing action. They remind Chris of a fabulous phrase he was introduced to by one of his guests, super-achiever August Turak, who had studied Zen Buddhism. The phrase is "Walk, not wobble."

Once they decide what they should do, follow-through masters don't wobble. They leave no success-wasting dead space between their good intentions and their actions.

If you're a follow-through master and you decide today that you should regularly review your advertising budget, or give feedback to your vendors, or survey your customers, or conduct spending reviews, or work on those performance appraisals that are due in a few weeks, that's all there is to it. You'll be ready to act boldly on your decision whether you feel like it or not.

Now, just in case the very idea of acting boldly on your intentions makes you a little nervous, let's be clear: Following through like a master has nothing to do with how you actually make decisions. It makes no difference whether you make decisions easily and quickly or only after agonizing over them forever; whether you rely mostly on logic or mostly on intuition; or whether you seek the opinions of others or prefer to fly solo. Whenever or however follow-through masters reach a decision, they act on it with focus, speed, and power, the way a hungry cheetah chases a gazelle.

It took Chris months to decide to run his first

teleseminar. He had never done anything like this before, and his mind was filled with doubts. What would people think? Would he be good at it? What if he failed? It took him a while to work his way through the doubts to a decision. But once he made the decision, he pulled the trigger and went full speed ahead.

> Whenever or however follow-through masters reach a decision, they act on it with focus, speed, and power.

Did it pay off? You bet it did! Chris was treated to a veritable feast of opportunities, including a chance to host what's become a wonderfully successful international radio show. What's more, his network of business contacts expanded by leaps and bounds, his personal profile got much taller, and his business achieved new heights.

Angie, Steve's client and the owner of a small home-based specialty e-commerce business, also got her gazelle. Her investment in developing exceptional follow-through skills paid off generously when she identified an opportunity for her business to break into a potentially lucrative new market. Angie evaluated the opportunity the same way she had always evaluated opportunities—cautiously. She thoroughly weighed and reweighed the risks, and she analyzed and reanalyzed the costs and possible rewards of jumping in. Although it was a close call, she eventually concluded that all things considered, she should go for it.

Before Angie had become a follow-through master, whenever she made a decision that was difficult to make, she either took forever to act on it, or she didn't act on it at all. But this time, as soon as she made the decision, she pulled the trigger. She acted boldly. As a result, she reported, sales nearly doubled.

Angie could always tell the difference between "I'm still trying to decide" and "I've already decided, but I'm just not acting on my decision." Although she still wobbles before she decides, she no longer wobbles after she decides. She walks. In fact, often she runs.

The ability to act swiftly and boldly on your decisions is not only an important asset, in today's rapid-paced business world it's getting to be a necessity. With accelerating advances in technology often giving rise to sudden new opportunities and sudden new threats, how ready you are to act on your decisions can make the difference between success and failure.

PUTTING IT INTO PRACTICE

1. What, if anything, do you currently do to try to make your intentions more effective?

2. What tasks or projects have you started with enthusiasm that left you flat before the job was done?

NOTES

CHAPTER 5

TAKING YOUR INTENTIONS SERIOUSLY

I am, indeed, a king, because I know how to rule myself.

—PIETRO ARETINO

You were probably taught how to read and write and do arithmetic, how to tie your shoelaces, and how to ride a bicycle and drive a car. But we'll venture a guess that you were never taught how to create serviceable good intentions and treat them in a way that maximizes their effectiveness.

In fact, we'll go even further out on a limb. We doubt that you've ever really thought much about what good intentions are and why they so often don't work.

You can improve your follow-through ability by taking your intentions more seriously—a whole lot more seriously. That means thinking about your intentions in a totally different way. It means being more aware, more deliberate, and more formal about the way you produce, adopt, and manage them.

One way to take your intentions more seriously is to think more thoroughly about what they are, what they represent, and how they can benefit you.

You can think of a good intention as a promise or a commitment you make to yourself to take an action that you've decided to take whether you feel like it or not. You can also think of a good intention as a *law*— not a law that others enacted and forced upon you, but one that you deliberately created, adopted, and enforce for your own benefit. You put the law in place because after thinking things through, you concluded that it was in your best interest to act in a certain way whether it's convenient or not. What's important here is that you passed the law *because* you knew there would be times that you wouldn't feel like doing what the law requires you to do. The law, in other words, recognizes that you might be tempted to stray, and it reminds you of the importance of staying on track.

We've been struck by how seriously the highly successful businesspeople we've worked with take their own intentions. They never take their intentions lightly. They're precise about what they intend to do. They think about their intentions explicitly and often. And they treat each intention like a solemn promise.

HOW TO MAKE THEM

A good intention should be a serious commitment to take a specific action that you believe will help you achieve a particular goal or objective. It's a promise you make to yourself to act in accord with a piece of good advice you've given yourself.

Suppose you've come to the conclusion that doing a better job of keeping up with the latest developments in your field will help you achieve your business, job, or career goals. All you've done so far is give yourself a piece of good advice. If you stop there and think you've created a serviceable good intention, you're wrong. Unless you really think things through and decide—

> Pseudo intentions are not only apt to fail, they stand to reduce the credibility and effectiveness of all your intentions.

we repeat, decide—to make a serious, explicit commitment to take your own good advice, your half-formed intention—if you can even call it that—is bound to fail.

Half-formed intentions—intentions that lack an explicit and robust "I've thought it through thoroughly and have decided to make a promise"—can actually do more harm than good. These pseudo intentions are not only apt to fail, they stand to reduce the credibility and effectiveness of all your intentions.

Skimping on the promise part of your intentions is like failing to do due diligence on a prospective business deal. Just because you can offer yourself a piece of good advice doesn't mean you should promise to take it. In fact you're far better off deciding not to take the advice than you are making a careless promise to follow it.

PROMISING LESS CAN ALLOW YOU TO DELIVER MORE

Taking your good intentions more seriously may mean adopting fewer intentions. It means deciding not to follow every single piece of advice you can give yourself. It means being thoughtful, thorough, deliberate, and selective—yes, *selective*—about the promises you make. It means adopting only fully formed intentions and never skimping on the "I promise" part. It means doing due diligence on your good advice before deciding whether to promise to follow it.

When it comes to good intentions, due diligence consists of more than just estimating the benefits of following your own advice. It includes taking into account all the likely obstacles and costs, such as the time and energy you'll have to divert from keeping other promises you've already made or those you may choose to make in the future.

So never allow a piece of advice you've given yourself—no matter how brilliant it may be—to masquerade as a serviceable intention. Unless you've thoroughly thought things through, decided that all things considered, this is truly a promise worth making, and you're ready and able to say under oath and in front of witnesses, "Yes, I will keep this promise," then please tell yourself in no uncertain terms, "This is good advice that I've decided not to take right now."

"I solemnly promise not to make so many promises."

Every time you prevent yourself from adopting a half-baked intention, you'll strengthen your follow-through ability. The more conscious, careful, deliberate, and formal you are about the "I promise" part of your intentions, the better job you'll do of actually behaving in accord with them.

Dr. Ivan Misner, chairman and founder of Business Networking International, who wrote the foreword for this book, knows all about being careful about the promises he makes. That's what helped him build the world's largest business networking organization.

"It's essential to focus on six things rather than a thousand," he insists.

We realize, of course, that we've made a very big deal about something that you normally do effortlessly without really thinking about it. Guess what? That's exactly why we're making such a big deal! Making promises to yourself *should be* a big deal! Making a practice of taking the "I promise" part of your intentions much more seriously is a big step in positioning your good intentions for success.

ELIMINATE WIGGLE ROOM

Making your intentions as specific as possible increases their effectiveness. That's why you should always try to eliminate as much *wiggle room* as possible. Leaving wiggle room—a lack of clarity about what exactly it is that you're promising to do—is an invitation for poor follow-through.

Let's again use the example of intending to do a better job of keeping up with the latest developments in your field. What exactly does "do a better job" mean? Unless you answer that question before you turn this "I really should" into an intention, you're weakening your chances of succeeding. To make this intention more effective, you need to be as specific as possible about what it is that you're promising to do. Instead of just promising to "do a better job," you could promise, for example, to "spend at least one hour a week reading about the latest developments."

Making your intentions more specific—eliminating wiggle room—makes you feel more accountable, and that will help you do what you intend to do.

Chris enjoyed great success when he started making a practice of eliminating wiggle room from his good intentions. For example, instead of settling for a vague intention like "I will lose weight," Chris got more specific. First he decided to focus more specifically on getting more exercise. But that wasn't specific enough. So he purchased a special electronic wristband and app that together counted and displayed how many steps he took every day. Then he promised, "I will take at least ten thousand steps every day." No wiggle room there! And when he decided he should do push-ups and sit-ups, he adopted "no wiggle room" intentions with the help of phone apps that gave him specific targets.

Remember, the more specific you make your intentions, the more accountable you'll feel for behaving in accord with them, and the more effective your intentions will be.

DON'T EXPECT YOUR INTENTIONS TO WORK AUTOMATICALLY

You probably regard self-confidence as a precious commodity. That's why we expect you to cringe when we tell you that one of the keys to doing what you intend to do is to get rid of any confidence you place in your natural ability to follow through.

Although we usually think of confidence as a good thing, confidence can be dangerous when what we're convinced is true just isn't. In fact, success sometimes depends on knowing when and how to ignore what you so confidently feel is true.

This is a lesson that airplane pilots must learn. Assuming that something is true just because it sure feels true can quite literally kill them. That's why as part of their training, student pilots must wear a special hood over their head that allows them to see the gauges and controls without also being able to see out the windows. The purpose of "hood work" is to teach pilots to rely on the instruments instead of what they sense or feel. The reason why this is so important is that when it comes to flying, what you so compellingly feel can be dangerously wrong.

"You have to trust your instruments—the facts in front of you—and not your feelings," said Mandy Hickson, a former Royal Air Force jet pilot who is now a professional speaker.

For example, as Mandy explained, your senses can fool you into believing that you're turning when, in fact, you've only stopped rolling. The confidence you feel won't change the truth. So to be a good pilot, you have to know when to distrust how you feel no matter how strongly you feel it.

We humans can be easily fooled by logic. We expect to follow through on our work-related good intentions because it's only logical that we would. Again, we want to succeed. We're motivated. We have dreams, and we definitely want to make them come true. Why wouldn't we do what we intend to do? Why shouldn't we be confident that we will?

That reflexive confidence that you'll automatically follow through is dangerous. It's about as reliable as the confidence of a student pilot who's ignoring what the instruments are trying to tell him. And trusting the confidence you feel can cause your good intentions to crash and burn.

Although intentions sure seem like they come with everything they need to be transformed into day-in, day-out action, they don't. They most definitely are not *self-implementing*. And any time you're confident that you'll just naturally do what you intend to do, you're making a big mistake.

It's not an easy thing to do, but it's a necessary thing to do: You have to make a point of ignoring the compelling but totally misleading feeling of confidence you get whenever you adopt an intention. When you reflexively think, "This is a great idea, so of course I'll do it," don't fall for it! Never count on doing what you intend to do unless you're willing to take another step. That step is developing and implementing a specific plan that lays out the

> Any time you're confident that you'll just naturally do what you intend to do, you're making a big mistake.

measures you'll take to make sure that you'll actually do what you intend to do.

WHAT YOU CAN LEARN FROM YOUR ALARM CLOCK

If developing a follow-through plan sounds a little too abstract or complicated, don't worry. If you've ever used an alarm clock to follow through on your intention to wake up at a certain time, you've already had experience developing a follow-through plan.

Suppose you intend to wake up at 4 a.m. tomorrow for an event you're really looking forward to attending. You're not only serious about getting up, you're enthusiastic about the reason for doing it. Still, you wouldn't just assume that having the intention is all it takes to implement it, would you? Of course not. Even though you're motivated, you'd take a second step. You'd use an alarm clock to prod you to do what

"I _really_ want to wake up
on time tomorrow."

you intend to do. Without the alarm clock, your intention alone—no matter how sincere it is—won't make you follow through.

A key to following through is, in a sense, to set an *alarm clock* for virtually every intention you adopt. You have to see to it that you'll be poked, prodded, pushed, coaxed, tricked, or forced to act in accord with each of your intentions.

In Chapter 10, we'll show you how to go about developing effective follow-through plans.

KEEP YOUR INTENTIONS IN THE SPOTLIGHT

To be effective, an intention must be at the very top of your mind. In other words, you must be actively aware of it. Unless you can keep your attention focused on what you intend to do, there's not much chance that you'll follow through.

No problem, right?

Wrong.

Staying focused on your intentions is a big challenge. Although it's only logical to assume that you'll pay attention to whatever you've decided is important, that's just not the way the normal human mind works. The truth is, our

> Your intentions—including the ones that have the greatest potential to make you successful—don't *automatically* stay at the top of your mind.

attention is often hijacked by things that don't matter at all. Meanwhile, our best intentions get lost in the shuffle.

Yes, as unfortunate as it is, it's a fact of life that your intentions—including the ones that have the greatest potential to make you successful—don't *automatically* stay at the top of your mind.

That's why one key to following through is to figure out how to stay actively aware of each of your good intentions. This can be a lot more difficult—and a whole lot more important—than you may think.

Steve discovered this principle over thirty years ago, and he attributes much of his own success in business to applying it.

In the early 1980s, Steve invented a simple electronic device called the MotivAider to help people do a better job of doing what they intended to do. Carried in a pocket or clipped to the user's waistband, the device used a silent pulsing vibration signal to automatically keep reminding the user to act on any chosen intention. Steve believed that by frequently capturing the user's attention and focusing it on a chosen intention, the MotivAider could prevent good intentions from getting lost in the shuffle.

Although Steve had absolutely no interest in business, he quickly realized that unless he could turn his idea into a tangible product that people could actually buy, his idea would have no chance of doing anyone any good.

Besides having no interest in business, Steve knew next to nothing about it. What's more, what little he did know, he didn't much like. But he realized that he would have to invest tons of time, energy, and money to have even a sliver of a sliver of a chance of succeeding. And he knew that being aware of the low probability that his efforts would result in success would only make it even more challenging to get and keep himself motivated to do all the difficult and unpleasant things he knew he would have to do.

So Steve gave himself lots of pep talks. But they didn't really do much good.

Then he came across a magazine article that he thought might motivate him. The article talked about cheetahs. It said that cheetahs catch only one out of ten gazelles they chase. But it pointed out that the only reason cheetahs ever get to dine on gazelle at all is that cheetahs essentially ignore the odds against them. They always run as fast as they can—as if they're going to catch dinner. If they took the odds against them seriously—the way we humans typically do—cheetahs probably wouldn't run as fast, and they would therefore never catch the occasional gazelle that makes the cheetah's business *profitable*.

Whenever he thought about it, Steve found the story quite inspiring. But before long, he rarely thought about it. Occasionally something would happen to remind him of the cheetah story, and whenever he remembered, he'd start acting more like a cheetah. But as soon as the story would fade from his mind—which it always did—he would act decidedly less cheetah-like.

Then it occurred to him: Why not use his own invention to keep the inspiring cheetah story at the very top of his mind? After all, he invented the MotivAider to enable people to automatically stay focused on any chosen good intention so they could do a better job of acting in accord with that intention. Steve truly intended to be more cheetah-like. He knew how to do it. He was motivated to do it. So he decided to give it a try.

Every time the pager-like MotivAider device sent Steve a signal in the form of a silent pulsing vibration, it reminded him to be like a cheetah—to ignore the odds stacked up against him and put all his might into everything he had to do to turn his idea into a successful business.

It made a huge difference right away. With the cheetah message going through his mind every few minutes all day long, instead of wasting his time, for example, thinking about whether it might be worthwhile to call so-and-so to see if he could possibly do such-and-such, Steve just called. And he kept on calling.

Before long, Steve had become a lean, mean success machine. He had made a habit of ignoring the odds against him, and by doing so, just like the cheetahs that inspired him, he had tilted the odds decidedly in his favor. And by making sure that his intention would stay at the top of his mind, Steve was able to keep on doing exactly what he intended to do.

CREATE INTENTION-ROUSING CUES

Let's look at the steps that Eve, the owner of a small retail business, took to keep her intention in the spotlight. After getting some unwelcome but constructive criticism from someone she trusted, Eve decided that from now on she'd make a practice of talking less and listening more to her customers. Although she was quite sincere about her intention, it somehow kept getting lost in the shuffle.

So Eve came up with a strategy to keep her attention focused on listening more. She set out to create a reminder—a cue—something tangible that would capture her attention and remind and urge her to listen instead of talk.

She found a large photo of an ear, wrote "Listen!" on it, placed it in an easel-type frame, and carefully positioned the picture on her desk where she would be sure to see it whenever she was speaking on the phone. Whenever she noticed her cue, it reminded and urged her to listen. In other words, the cue helped arouse an intention that would otherwise have been inactive.

Unfortunately, after a while, Eve was no longer consistently noticing her cue.

Eve learned that it was quite challenging to keep her cue noticeable enough to do the job of keeping her intention at the top of her mind. So whenever her cue started to fade into the background, she had to do something to change it enough to make it noticeable again.

Like Eve, you've probably had the experience before of something that initially captured your attention but then soon started to fade into the background. Maybe, for example, there was a poster on the wall that inspired you when you first saw it, but now, even though it's still there, it's pretty much invisible. That's perfectly normal and also perfectly predictable, which is why it's essential to always find a way to keep cues noticeable.

When Eve exchanged her ear photo for a MotivAider, she associated the message "Listen" with the MotivAider's vibration signal so that whenever she felt the MotivAider vibrate, she automatically thought, "Listen!" Unlike the ear photo that reminded her to listen only when she happened to notice it, the MotivAider's vibration signal worked like a tap on the shoulder to get Eve's attention and keep her focused on listening. Thanks to frequent private taps on the shoulder from her MotivAider, Eve was able to build a solid habit of listening more and speaking less.

If you don't have a MotivAider or a mobile phone with a MotivAider app installed, don't worry. You can still make use of the MotivAider concept. Just use anything that's capable of sending you frequent signals. The trick is to assign a motivating meaning—a personal message—to the signal so that whenever you get the signal, you also get the motivating message that urges you to take the desired action.

By the way, although you can use a cue to remind yourself simply of a specific action you intend to take, you may get even better results if you use a cue to remind yourself of a motivating *why* behind your intention.

Jo Simpson, a professional speaker, always tries to keep her attention focused on the why—the purpose—behind the various tasks she needs to do. "This makes me super productive," she told us. "When I don't do it, I'm definitely not as driven."

David Hyner, a professional communicator, told us that he keeps a picture of his son at eye level where he can't miss it. Whenever he notices it, it reminds him of his *Big Why*.

Chris tries to stay focused on the Big Whys behind everything he does. He's constantly experimenting with cues that can keep his attention focused on the purposes that he wants to drive him the most. He's learned that even his potentially most powerful whys—like wanting to set the finest example he possibly can for his children and clients, wanting to be able to look back during his twilight years with pride at his accomplishments, wanting to act on his dreams now because life is too short and unpredictable to wait for later, wanting to leave a legacy—won't automatically stay at the top of his mind. And he's learned that finding creative ways to keep his attention focused on these Big Whys is the best way to empower them to drive success-producing action.

One thing that works well for Chris is a great big whiteboard that sits on the wall right in front of his desk. His first task each day is updating it, and he's managed to make this more or less a matter of habit. There's a lot on the board. There are various to-do items and a graph showing his financial progress. But there's also the really important stuff: a list of his Big Whys, a list of his intentions, and some quotes that remind Chris of his priorities and values.

PUTTING IT INTO PRACTICE

1. Are your work-related intentions specific enough? If not, how can you make them more specific?

2. Which intentions need to be fortified, and which, if any, should you consider ditching?

3. Are there any intentions not directly related to your work that have a bearing on your work performance? If so, what are they?

4. What assumptions have you been making about how your intentions will work?

5. What assumptions should you make from now on?

6. How might you use the alarm clock concept to make a particular good intention more effective?

7. Think of a good intention you have, and devise a way to keep your attention focused on it. Now try this with as many good intentions as you think could benefit from being in the spotlight.

NOTES

_____
_____
_____
_____
_____
_____
_____
_____
_____
_____
_____
_____
_____
_____
_____
_____
_____
_____
_____
_____
_____
_____
_____
_____

CHAPTER 6

HOW TO GIVE YOUR INTENTIONS ALL THE POWER THEY NEED

Necessity is the mother of follow-through.

—STEVE LEVINSON AND PETE GREIDER, *FOLLOWING THROUGH*

To do a particular thing you intend to do but don't feel like doing, you need to be able to put enough power behind your good intention to overcome that "I don't wanna do it!" feeling in your gut that pushes back when your intention tries to push you forward. Naturally, the more resistance or reluctance you feel, the more power it will take to do what you intend to do. So the trick to following through is knowing how to put more power behind your intention and/or how to put less resistance in front of it.

MAKE IT FEEL NECESSARY

Think about some of the extraordinary people you've heard about who faced enormous obstacles but simply refused to accept the odds against them. They just kept pressing forward, often doing extremely difficult things day in and day out without getting even the slightest result to encourage them. They went on like this for months or even years. And then suddenly, they achieved success.

What's their secret? How did they make themselves do it?

Well, many of the super-achievers we've encountered did it because, in a sense, they had no choice. They felt like they *had to* do it. They felt driven to do anything and everything they believed they needed to do in order to succeed.

Take Chris's friend Billy Schwer. Billy spent twenty years in arguably the most grueling and demanding sport there is—boxing. During his impressive career, Billy won British, Commonwealth, European, and International boxing organization world titles. His skills, courage, determination, and grace in the ring attracted a huge fan base, and his personality made him a favorite among other boxers, promoters, and the media.

So what was the secret that enabled Billy to stick with the rigorous training regimen that was so critical to his success? Billy's secret was that *he felt like he had no choice.*

"If I didn't train in the rain, sleet, or snow," he told Chris, "I knew there was a big risk I would get killed in the ring!"

So it wasn't just a matter of *thinking* he really should stick with his training regimen. Billy could actually feel it in his gut: *Train or die!*

Then there's Meryl Koslow, a successful entrepreneur who spent years *wiring* herself to follow through as if she were shot out of a cannon.

"I am always motivated," Meryl told Chris. "I have firecrackers in me when I wake up. All I want is to make millions of dollars in every given minute, and I feel driven to do it."

MOTIVATION FOR THE REST OF US

Most of us don't have firecrackers in us when we wake up. And most of us don't feel like we'll literally be killed unless we do what we know we should do every day. For every Meryl and Billy who is lucky enough to automatically feel a compulsion to do whatever he or she believes success requires, there are millions of ambitious, hardworking people like us who just aren't wired that way. Although we truly want to succeed, we don't automatically feel like we must do the things we know will make us successful.

But just because you're not wired the way Billy and Meryl are, that doesn't mean you can't follow through like them. It just means that you have to do something *manually* that they do *automatically*. It means you have to learn how to become deliberate and creative about making yourself feel like doing what you know you must do to be successful.

Of course, it would be nice if it would just happen automatically. But that's not going to happen, so here's our advice: *Get over it!* The worst thing you can do is pretend that you're wired like Billy and Meryl if you're not.

> Trick yourself into actually feeling— not just thinking— like you *must* do the same thing you've decided you should do.

The secret to following through is to essentially *trick yourself* into actually feeling—not just thinking—like you *must* do the same thing you've decided you should do.

Alastair Campbell, who is head of the Ideal Marketing Company, figured out a way to make himself feel like he had to lose weight. He wrote out a check for £500 (about $800) to a political party that he really disliked. He then gave the check to a trusted friend with instructions to mail the check unless Alastair had lost at least 9.5 kilograms (about 21 pounds) by "weigh in" at the end of October.

It wasn't just money that Alastair put on the line. He realized that if he didn't lose the weight and the donation was therefore made in his company's name, his company would appear on a list of staunch supporters of an organization he found totally repulsive. Imagine how embarrassing that would be!

So Alastair, who couldn't lose the weight for all the *right* reasons, lost the weight to keep from losing his money and his honor.

GOING TOO FAR?

Now, if you think Alastair went too far, think again.

Just imagine what you could accomplish by creating high-octane reasons like this that actually force you to do the various things you intend to do. For example, suppose you've intelligently decided that you really should make an important call that you've been putting off. Or suppose you really should work on that financial spreadsheet that you should have finished two weeks ago. If the good and right and logical reasons for doing these things just aren't working, seriously, why wouldn't you be willing to get yourself in gear by taking the kind of extreme measure that Alastair took?

When the right reason for doing something important doesn't work, what's wrong with creating a compelling reason that does work? You see, if you have the stomach for it, you can always create a compelling reason that's powerful enough to force you to do what you intend to do.

> You can always create a compelling reason that's powerful enough to force you to do what you intend to do.

Ironically, the biggest obstacle you have to overcome in order to put this principle into practice is an irresistibly logical and widely held belief that's dead wrong. It's the belief that you can and should count only on the good or the right reasons for doing what you intend to do to motivate you to actually follow through.

We urge you to forget about whatever you think should motivate you. All that matters is what actually does motivate you. A good or right reason that fails to make you feel in your gut like you absolutely must do what you've decided you should do is useless. You're much better off with a bad or wrong or dumb or irrelevant reason that nevertheless makes you feel like you must do what you intend to do.

Billy Schwer, who never beats around the bush, put it this way: "Whatever will empower you, you must use it to get yourself off your arse."

Of course, you should always *decide* to follow through for the right reasons. But it's a huge mistake to count on the right reasons to also make you actually do what you intend to do. To do what you intend to do, you need a compelling reason—that is, one that you can actually feel rather than just think. And if you don't have a compelling reason, you have no choice but to create one. That not only takes practice, it takes courage.

TAKE A LESSON FROM THE MARKETING INDUSTRY

Are you amazed at how little effort you're sometimes willing to put forth to achieve a result you truly want to achieve? Well, it's only human nature to, shall we say, *conserve effort*. William Moore captured this unfortunate truth in his book, *On Character and Mental Toughness*. "Never underestimate the capacity of people to choose the easy way," he wrote.

It's discouraging. What could possibly be good about the realization that your good intentions—the intelligent decisions you make about what's best for you—can be so fragile that all it takes to break them is having to put forth the slightest amount of effort?

Well, are you ready to be pleasantly surprised? Hidden within that sad truth is a powerful idea that will unleash follow-through power you never knew you had.

You see, if you play your cards right, you can turn

> Make it harder to violate your intention and easier to do what you intend to do.

your usually troublesome inclination to conserve effort into a valuable asset that will actually help you do what you intend to do.

A powerful key to following through is to make it harder to violate your intention and easier to do what you intend to do.

Interestingly, the marketing industry knows all about this particular follow-through concept. In fact, they use it quite cleverly to increase their profits at our expense.

In the United States, mail-in rebates are a common way for companies to stimulate sales of their products. The way rebates work is pretty simple. A company encourages you to buy their product by promising to give you some of your money back after you make the purchase. For example, a company might offer a $100 rebate if you purchase a television that normally costs $500. By offering a lower final price, the company reduces the resistance consumers have to buying, so more consumers buy. But here's the catch: To get your money back, you typically have to fill out a form, send it along with other required documentation to the company's agent, and then wait several weeks to get your check.

Now, if that doesn't seem like much of a catch to you, it's because you haven't noticed how much people *conserve effort*! It turns out that as few as 10 percent of the consumers who buy a product *because* of the rebate ever actually put forth the objectively small (but apparently subjectively large) amount of effort required to get the rebate.

Offering rebates is a brilliant business strategy. It allows a company to increase its sales and profits by offering a discount that it knows many, if not most, of its customers won't actually get. But the strategy is based on a keen insight about human nature: *We're more likely to do things that feel easy. And we're less likely to do things that feel hard.* Businesses offering a rebate ideally want you to buy their product and not claim the rebate. So they make it feel easy to buy and hard to get your money back.

You can use this insight to improve your ability to follow through. All you have to do is structure things so that it's easier to do what you intend to do than it is to not do it.

Steve used this insight to follow through on his good intention to stop snacking on a food he loved.

One day, while grocery shopping, Steve tasted a sample of Genoa salami. It was love at first taste. He was smitten. After some discussion, he and his wife selected a good-sized chunk of the delicious salami and had it sliced at the store. They then took it home, placed it in the refrigerator, and decided it would be reserved for meals.

Yeah, right.

Steve couldn't get anywhere near the refrigerator

without hearing the salami call his name. And whenever he was called, he *answered*. It was so easy. Just grab a slice, or two, or three. All he had to do was open the refrigerator door, reach into a plastic bag, and grab some. He didn't need a knife. He didn't need a dish. The slices seemed to jump into his hand. It couldn't have been easier.

Steve never took or ate a slice of that salami without first remembering his good intention. But still, he snacked and snacked and snacked until the salami was gone.

He thought a lot about why his good intention wimped out. What a weakling that intention was! But then it dawned on him. He had weakened his own intention by making it so easy to violate it. He realized that he should have made it harder to do the wrong thing.

So when the salami was gone, Steve decided to make "conservation of effort" work in his favor. He went back to the store and bought some more salami, but this time, he made a point of *not* having it sliced at the store. Instead, he brought a big chunk of it home and put it in the fridge.

What a difference! The salami still called his name, but instead of answering, Steve thought about what he'd have to do to get some of that delicious salami. He'd have to get a knife and a cutting board, both of which he'd have to wash after he used them. He'd also have to peel back the wrapping material, which didn't come off very easily. It all seemed like an awful lot of work to him. Maybe he didn't need to have a piece of salami after all.

By making it harder to violate his intention, Steve made his intention stronger—strong enough, in fact, to make him do what he actually intended to do.

But wait, it gets even better. Not only was he repelled by *the hard work* he'd have to do to snack on the salami he really wanted, he was attracted by the ease with which he could just take an apple (which he had cleverly placed right next to the salami) instead, which is what he ended up doing.

Make it hard to do   Make it easy to do
the wrong thing.   the right thing.

Kyle used a similar approach to solve a problem at work.

A customer services supervisor for a small telemarketing company, Kyle was scheduled to meet monthly on a one-to-one basis with each of the dozen customer services representatives he supervised. Having the meetings was Kyle's idea. He had started the tradition because he was convinced that meeting regularly with each of his reps would contribute to higher levels of performance, help prevent morale problems, and make it possible to identify and address personnel problems early on.

Although Kyle maintained his belief in the value of these individual meetings, he didn't much enjoy them. In fact, he nearly always groaned when he noticed one of these meetings on his daily schedule. About a third of the time, he would ask his secretary to cancel the meeting.

Although he always had some justification for canceling, Kyle wasn't really fooling himself. He realized that he often exaggerated the importance or urgency of competing responsibilities just so that he could make it okay to cancel a meeting he didn't feel like having. He wasn't happy with himself at all. He gave himself speeches, reminded himself of the important purpose behind the meetings, and promised himself repeatedly that he'd stop canceling them. But Kyle's promises were no match for the groans he made when he looked at his schedule.

Frustrated and disappointed, Kyle was finally ready to abandon the hope that his good intention alone would keep him on track. It was time to take the bull by the horns.

So Kyle went to his secretary and let her know what he was trying to accomplish and why. He told her that from now on, if he had to cancel a meeting with any of his reps, he would do it himself. She would be responsible only for making the appointments and putting them in his schedule—never for canceling them.

Kyle knew that he would feel reluctant to call reps himself to cancel their meetings. Although he had obviously already done plenty of canceling, he had been able to do it the easy way—that is, by simply asking his secretary to do it. Having to do it himself would be much harder—hard enough that he was sure he'd want to avoid doing it. It would just be easier, he figured, to have the meeting even if he didn't feel like it.

Kyle was right. By deliberately making it harder to cancel the meetings than to have them, he gave his intention the power it needed.

NEVER RELY UNNECESSARILY ON WILLPOWER

Have you ever asked yourself what willpower is? Would you agree that it's basically a measure of your ability to do what you believe you should do when you don't feel like doing it?

The less you feel like working on a task you intend to work on, the more willpower it will take for you to do it. Willpower is like physical strength. The heavier an object is—the more it resists—the more physical strength you'll need to lift it on your own. The more you dread doing a particular task, the more willpower you'll need to get that task done.

If you take the analogy a step further, you'll be

rewarded with an important insight that can do wonders for your follow-through ability.

You see, we've developed all kinds of tools that make it possible for us to lift heavy objects—to overcome resistance—with very little physical strength. For example, if you have a flat tire, you don't have to rely on brute strength to lift your car. With the right tool, a tire jack, you can use a very small amount of physical strength to get a very large result. The trick is in applying your strength in the right way.

In a sense, the same is true of your willpower. How much you can accomplish with it depends less on how much willpower you have than it does on how you apply it.

Just as you'd be foolish to rely on your physical strength alone to lift a car, you'd be foolish to rely on your willpower alone to get yourself to do a task that you dread doing. What's more, beating yourself up for not having enough willpower makes as much sense as beating yourself up for being too physically weak to lift a car with your bare hands.

USE YOUR WILLPOWER WISELY

It's worth repeating: How successful you are in doing what you intend to do depends less on how much willpower you have than it does on how wisely you use the willpower you have.

Allow us to use an admittedly far-fetched example to make this important point.

John, who has been hopelessly addicted to cigarettes since he was an adolescent, has just decided to quit smoking. This is the seventeenth time in the last ten years that he's decided to quit.

If John continues to have easy access to cigarettes, it will take an extraordinary amount of willpower for him to resist the urge to smoke. He'll have to draw on his willpower many times each day to fight the temptation to smoke. And even if he wins the occasional battle, there's a good chance that he'll once again lose the war.

So what if we could offer John an opportunity to pull a lever that would make cigarettes totally inaccessible to him from now on no matter how desperately he wants to smoke? All he would have to do is pull the lever once, and John would never again be able to get a cigarette.

So all John would need is enough willpower to make himself pull the lever. After that, he wouldn't need willpower anymore because cigarettes wouldn't be available to him no matter how desperately he wanted to smoke. John would follow through on his "quit smoking" intention—not because he had extraordinary willpower, but because he was smart enough to pull a lever that made it unnecessary for him to have extraordinary willpower.

Of course, there's probably no practical way for John to make it literally impossible for himself to access cigarettes. But any action that he can take to at least make it more difficult to get hold of a cigarette when he feels like smoking will reduce the amount of willpower he'll need to resist the urge, and that will increase his chances of doing what he intends to do.

Relying as little as possible on willpower is an extremely important follow-through principle. Always be on the lookout for ways to create *levers* that make it possible for you to do what you know you should do without using any more willpower than necessary.

Gabriela, a manager for a small shipping company, created a lever that allowed her to solve a problem she couldn't solve by relying on her willpower. After struggling unsuccessfully many times a day to act in accord with her intention to stop wasting so much time fussing with her smartphone at work, she decided to stop relying on willpower to get the job done. She exchanged her smartphone for a dumb phone and a tablet, and she left the tablet at home and brought only the dumb phone to work. Problem solved!

Chris relies on a lever to reduce the amount of willpower he needs to follow through on his intention to get physical exercise. His lever is a Labradoodle named Barney. Although he can't count on his willpower, Chris can always count on Barney to give him one of those irresistible "Please take me for a walk" looks. It works *nearly* every time. (We know, Barney, he slipped up a few times.) Even when it's raining or snowing or he doesn't really feel like going for a walk, thanks to Barney, Chris almost always gets the exercise he intends to get without having to rely on the willpower he usually lacks.

OUTSMART TEMPTATION

When Chris's son Daniel was four years old, he couldn't resist the temptation to give himself a haircut. Although the result was horrifying to his parents, nobody really expects a four-year-old to anticipate and be guided by the likely consequences of his or her actions. We don't really expect young children to be experts in resisting temptation.

We do, however, expect responsible serious-minded adults to resist temptations both large and small. But, frankly, even adults aren't very good at resisting temptations. Look at all the smart politicians and others who ruin their careers by giving in to temptation. Look at all of us who can't resist the temptation to "just quickly check something on the Internet" instead of sticking with the work we intend to do. Fighting temptation is never easy. But it's a lot easier if you fight smart.

The smartest way to beat temptation is the way that

requires the least amount of willpower. So if you can, get rid of the temptation completely. And if you can't do that, then eliminate the opportunity to do what you're tempted to do. And if you can't do that, either, then at least make it as difficult as possible for you to do what you're tempted to do.

> Fighting temptation is never easy. But it's a lot easier if you fight smart.

Honestly, it's plain foolish to rely on willpower to fight battle after battle when you can just take one smart action now to end the war.

Nicci Roscoe is a lifestyle and corporate coach, former TV fitness expert, creator of *Fabulous Impact*, and brain tumor survivor who's made a solid commitment to eating healthy. She's trained herself to look at every food item she's about to eat and ask herself, "Will this contribute to my health or detract from it?" If it will contribute, she eats it. If it will detract, she decides not to.

Although Nicci has amazing drive, she's smart enough not to waste willpower. Why rely on willpower when she can take a smart, simple action that makes willpower unnecessary? That's why after struggling to resist the temptation to eat the yummy Kit Kat in her fridge, Nicci asked her daughter to "just take it away." That easily solved the problem and allowed Nicci to save her willpower for a job that really required it.

"For some reason I find it hard to
resist the temptation to eat cookies."

Steve's client Michael, a small business owner
with big dreams, kept trying to use his willpower to
resist the temptation to sketch out floor plans for a
new building that he hoped his business would someday be able to build and afford. He recognized that by
spending so much time daydreaming, he was preventing himself from doing the real work he had to do
in order to actually have a shot at making his dream
come true. Still, he was rarely able to resist the temptation to spend "just a few more minutes" manipulat-
ing the plans on his computer screen. Unfortunately,
more often than not, "just a few more minutes" turned
into an hour or more.

Michael was horrified whenever he thought about
how much time and effort he was wasting. Yet his frequent self-scoldings didn't do any good, and neither
did the mounting hard evidence that his failure to
stay focused on important work was beginning to
hurt his business.

Finally, after learning about follow-through strategies, Michael was ready to take the bull by the horns. He deleted the floor plan design program from his computer, transferred his dream files to a memory stick, and put the memory stick on a top shelf in a storage closet outside his office.

Although Michael's desire to spend time revising the floor plans didn't go away, the opportunity did. Every once in a while, he felt really tempted to go fetch the memory stick. But as soon as he started thinking about having to reinstall the software, he dropped the idea and got back to doing the real work he intended to do.

There is another way to outsmart temptation. It's based on the observation that sometimes you can weaken a temptation by offering to *partly* give in to it. This can be especially useful when there's no practical way to completely get rid of a temptation.

The idea is to give yourself permission to actually do the wrong (tempting) thing as long you do a little bit of a right thing first.

Jane, a buyer for a large variety store chain, struggled to resist the temptation to shop for personal items on the Internet when she should have been working. This was bothering her enough that had she had the option, she would have gladly taken steps to make it impossible for her to shop. Unfortunately, that option wasn't available, because shopping—although obviously not shopping for personal items—was part of Jane's job.

So Jane had to come up with a different approach. She made a deal with herself. If she felt tempted to shop for personal items, instead of scolding herself and trying as hard as possible to resist, which is what she had been doing, she would allow herself to shop *but only after* spending at least a few minutes working on a project that was on her to-do list.

Jane noticed a couple of things right away that surprised her. First of all, once she agreed to partially give in to the temptation, the temptation became noticeably tamer. Secondly, often when she put off shopping for personal items to honor her commitment to briefly work first on a project, she just kept working on the project. Jane was no longer feeling guilty, and she was getting more work done.

LET SITUATIONS DO THE HEAVY LIFTING

Suppose you want to discourage people from entering a particular room that you know from experience passersby will want to enter. Which of these two methods do you think would be the most effective in keeping people out?

a. Put a sign on the door that says "Do Not Enter."

b. Skip the sign, but keep the door locked!

The best way to get people to conform to a rule is to make it impossible for them to break the rule. If you can't make it impossible, at least make it as hard as possible. "Speed bumps" on streets work better than signs do to get motorists to slow down. Railroad crossing gates work better than flashing lights to get motorists to stop. If you want a little boy to stop terrorizing his sister with his water pistol, you'd be better off taking the water pistol away from him than insisting *again and again and again* that he stop.

> Situations that *force* people to do the right thing work better than efforts to *persuade* them to do the right thing.

The point is, situations that *force* people to do the right thing work better than efforts to *persuade* them to do the right thing.

Why not apply that same point to your own good intentions?

Whenever you can, rely on situations to do the heavy lifting. The most airtight way to see to it that you'll do what you intend to do is to create a situation that *forces* you to do it—that leaves you feeling like you have no choice.

Jamal created a situation to force himself to do something he knew he should do but just wasn't doing.

A partner in a small business that offered music lessons, Jamal kept trying and failing to act in accord with his good intention to closely monitor his business's Google AdWords campaign. He had set up the campaign himself and was an enthusiastic advocate

"I've never felt so motivated!"

for using this type of targeted web advertising to get new business. The campaign was working quite well, but Jamal was acutely aware of the need to closely monitor and tweak it to maximize its cost-effectiveness, which is why he was so frustrated by his failure to stick with his intention.

So Jamal asked his partner and their assistant to come to his office every Wednesday morning at 10 a.m. for a Google AdWords results meeting. He figured that having them come there explicitly for that purpose would force him to do the weekly monitoring he wasn't doing. But Jamal didn't stop there. He added another layer of follow-through insurance just for good measure. With his partner's full support, Jamal made a point at each meeting of setting the campaign to automatically stop running in a week. That meant that unless he logged in to his AdWords account, the campaign would stop, and his business would lose its most valuable source of referrals. What's more, it would be Jamal's fault, and his partner would know it.

Nothing will guarantee follow-through better than a situation that leaves you feeling as if you have no choice but to do what you intend to do.

PUTTING IT INTO PRACTICE

1. Can you think of examples where you relied on "a good reason" that just didn't push you hard enough to get the job done?

2. How might you have created a compelling reason to make your intention more effective?

3. How can you use "conservation of effort" to help you do something you intend to do?

4. If you've used levers before, how did you use them and what did they help you accomplish?

5. How might a lever help you turn any of your current intentions into action?

6. What are some temptations and distractions that detract from your ability to be as successful as you'd like to be, and what ideas do you have for outsmarting them?

7. Are there situations or circumstances that force you to follow through?

8. What situations or circumstances could you create to get yourself to act on a particularly important intention?

NOTES

_____

_____

_____

_____

_____

_____

_____

_____

_____

_____

_____

_____

_____

_____

_____

_____

_____

_____

PART THREE

Smart Strategies for Getting Things Done

Most powerful is he who has himself in his own power.

—SENECA

_____

In this section, we'll rely chiefly on real-life examples to demonstrate smart strategies that you can use to get things done whether you feel like it or not.

CHAPTER 7

TURN UP THE HEAT

What may be done at any time will be done at no time.

—SCOTTISH PROVERB

If you own your own business or have a job that gives you a fair amount of room to do things your own way, you probably value your freedom. You probably don't like feeling confined, restricted, pressured, or forced. That's why you'll find it ironic that some of the most effective follow-through strategies sound like a list of torture techniques that were specially designed for freedom-lovers.

How about deliberately locking yourself in a cage? Or deliberately hanging yourself by your tongue? Or deliberately burning a bridge behind you?

Why in the world would we suggest that you do any of these horrible freedom-robbing things to yourself? The answer is simple: Because they work! Whenever you deliberately put yourself in a jam that you

121

can only get out of by doing what you intend to do, you're using a smart follow-through strategy—one that works by making you actually feel like you must do what you intend to do.

"We're carrying out your strict orders not to allow you out until you've cleared your desk."

LOCK YOURSELF IN A CAGE

In 2011, Chris decided to lock himself in a cage—figuratively speaking, of course. He made a commitment to produce a weekly radio show. This wasn't just a promise he made to himself. His commitment included signing a legal contract, putting some money on the line, and generating some pretty high expectations on the part of family members, friends, colleagues, and clients.

When Chris pulled the "I commit" lever, he had no idea just how much of his time and effort this project would end up requiring. And that's a good thing, because if he had known, he never would have pulled that lever. And if he hadn't, Chris and his business would have been deprived of the extraordinary benefits they're now enjoying.

By pulling the "I commit" lever, Chris leveraged his willpower to the max. He placed himself in a situation that made him feel like he had no choice but to do success-producing things he often didn't feel like doing. Being in the cage meant he didn't have to spend valuable willpower to get himself in gear to prepare for each radio show. The commitment he'd already made took care of that. If he even considered letting things slide, Chris was immediately bombarded by intensely unpleasant thoughts and feelings about the horrible consequences of slacking off. And that was enough to get him moving forward—whether he felt like it or not.

So pulling the "I commit" lever is the secret behind Chris's ability to keep on doing an extraordinary amount of extremely productive work.

In just three years, Chris managed to record more than 140 interviews, which is especially impressive when you consider the extensive research that each interview required.

Chris is utterly convinced the he could never have been this productive without the friendly pressure he unleashed by pulling the "I commit" lever.

Since learning about the value of the lever, he makes a point of pulling it often. He doesn't do it because he enjoys the pressure, but because he enjoys the benefits of doing what he intends to do. Although he still cherishes the freedom to choose his own goals and objectives, Chris has learned that freedom from pressure can actually be the enemy of follow-through; that by willingly locking himself in a cage, he can achieve truly amazing things that would never be possible if he avoided rather than welcomed pressure.

Here are just some of the benefits of following through that Chris now enjoys:

- His radio show is heard in more than fifty countries.
- He's in high demand as a mentor, facilitator, speaker, and interviewer.
- He has an exponentially growing list of international clients.
- His clients can benefit from knowledge and wisdom he gleans by interacting with experts and amazing personalities from around the globe.
- Companies use his radio show to educate their employees and customers.
- He's featured in such magazines as *Small Business Owner* and is increasingly sought after for interviews.
- Relationships he's developed with many of the guests on his radio show have opened up opportunities for joint ventures and resulted in exposure to important new networks.
- He's amassed a huge library of content he can

use to create high-value books and other
products.

- He's developed highly efficient methods to
create and market his shows.

HANG YOURSELF BY YOUR TONGUE

If there were such a thing as a Follow-Through Hall of
Fame, Andy McMenemy's portrait would surely be
prominently displayed there. Imagine this: In 2011, he
ran 66 ultra-marathons in 66 consecutive days in 66
cities! What's more, he did this despite crippling inju-
ries and unrelenting pain.

So how in the world did Andy manage to follow
through? He attributes his success in part to a strategy
he aptly calls "Hung by Your Tongue."

"Once I declare to the world that I'm going to do
it," Andy told us, "I feel like I have to do it!"

Yes, there's nothing like the follow-through power
you can create by making the right *public* promise—a
promise you feel (not just think) you absolutely must
keep.

Steve and Pete Greider managed to harness that
power to ensure that they would finish writing their
book, *Following Through*, even though sometimes (okay,
often) they didn't really feel like writing. By making a
point of announcing to their colleagues, friends, and
clients that they would be writing a book about, of all
things, how to follow through, they locked themselves

in a cage that they couldn't get out of without getting the job done.

Susan Alexander, a successful property coach and investor, recognizes the awesome power she can create simply by making a promise she feels she must keep. That's why she promises her nephews and nieces that she will give them treats as soon as she completes a project she intends to finish. The very thought of having to inform her nephews and nieces that they won't be getting the promised treats because their aunt is a slacker makes her feel like she absolutely must do what she intends to do.

If you're thinking that it's just not logical that Susan would be moved more by the fear of breaking a promise to her nephews and nieces than by the fear of breaking a promise to herself, you're right. It's not logical. But that doesn't matter. What matters to Susan is what works for Susan. And what should matter to you is what works for you.

BURN YOUR BRIDGES BEHIND YOU

Kathy Tracey was a member of a four-woman crew that held a world record for being the first ever to successfully cross an ocean in a rowing boat. During their sixty-seven-day ordeal across the Atlantic, the crew had to endure gale force winds, treacherous seas, lost communication, and illness and injury.

Not surprisingly, Kathy often gets asked if they felt

like giving up. Of course, they felt like giving up! So why didn't they?

"Once we got started," Kathy explains, "giving up ceased to be an option . . . unless we wanted to swim home!"

Yes, sometimes the best way to get yourself to go forward is by removing the opportunity to go backward.

> Sometimes the best way to get yourself to go forward is by removing the opportunity to go backward.

Twice world champion single skulls rower Mette Bloch, who's now a successful TV presenter and professional speaker, used this strategy to finally make good on her intention to perform as a stand-up comedian. Instead of just continuing to wait for the day when she'd be able to muster up enough courage to venture way outside her comfort zone and pursue her dream, she decided that the way for her to go forward was by burning a bridge behind her.

So Mette went ahead and booked a 1,635-seat conference hall for her first performance as a comedian. Booking the hall way in advance made it easier for Mette to burn the bridge. Still, once she paid the non-refundable rental fee of £14,000 (about $21,000), things felt decidedly different.

Mette, of course, knew exactly what she was doing. By deliberately putting herself in a situation in which she would feel even worse about retreating than about advancing, she knew she would go forward. She now felt like she had no choice, which is exactly what she wanted. She still felt quite apprehensive about performing. But because she now felt even more apprehensive about the possibility of irresponsibly squandering her hard-earned money, she followed through.

By the way, the tickets to Mette's performance completely sold out. She gave a great performance, and she was delighted with her success. So bravo, Mette, and kudos to the awesome power of deliberately putting yourself in a jam that you can't get out of without doing what you intend to do.

After hearing Steve speak about this strategy, Lisa, a professional organizer, decided to burn a bridge behind her in order to force herself to finally follow through on her intention to paint her office.

Lisa had picked out the color and bought the paint months before, but she just kept putting off painting because she didn't feel like doing it. Scolding herself for not following through hadn't helped, but she finally had an idea. She grabbed a can of paint and a brush and slopped some paint on the most visible wall in her office.

She had taken an action that would make her feel like she had to go forward. The paint smeared on the wall left her with no choice but to finish the job. If she left the mess the way it was, she knew that her clients would see it and might well question—perhaps justifiably!—whether Lisa was really qualified to help them get organized. So she followed through because she now felt like she *had to* do what she intended to do.

An attendee at one of Chris's presentations was inspired to deliberately put herself in a jam that she could get out of only by doing something she intended to do but dreaded doing. Although she had long ago unequivocally reached the conclusion that she should quit her job, she kept putting off resigning because she dreaded having to deal with her employer's reaction. Although she gave herself many speeches about the importance of just going ahead and doing the deed, the speeches didn't help.

"Even though I knew I had to do it, I just couldn't muster up the courage to do it," she said.

Finally, she saw the light. She realized that the only way for her to stop avoiding doing the deed was to deliberately take action to make it feel even worse to *not* go forward than it felt to go forward. So she wrote a resignation letter and gave it to a trusted colleague with strict instructions to deliver it to her employer on a certain date. She still dreaded her employer's reaction, but now she dreaded even more the reaction she would get to a resignation letter that had to be delivered by someone else because she was just too much of a chicken to deliver it herself! Now that it finally *felt necessary* to do what she intended to do, she did it.

MAKE THE CONSEQUENCES FEEL REAL

It's not enough for the consequences of not doing what you intend to do to be real. You have to make them *feel* real.

In *Following Through*, Levinson and Greider cite a number of examples of people who followed through by making the consequences of not following through *feel real*.

Jeff, who started his own insurance business, was puzzled by his failure to keep a promise he had made to himself. After attending an inspiring sales conference, Jeff had made a commitment to make ten cold sales calls a week to prospective clients. He made the commitment because he was utterly convinced that making the calls would help him achieve his business goals. He was confident that he'd follow through and baffled when he didn't.

Then Jeff learned about what it really takes to follow through. He accepted the fact that even though there was no doubt in his mind that making these cold calls was the right thing to do to achieve the success he so badly wanted, he just didn't feel a strong enough push in his gut to do something that he hated to do.

So Jeff set out to create a situation in which he would actually feel like he *must* make "those damned cold calls."

Here's the situation he created: Each time his assistant would make her weekly trip to the bank to make deposits, she would get a hundred dollars in cash—ten ten-dollar bills. She would put the money—Jeff's money—in an envelope marked "Jeff's Cold Calls" and keep the envelope in a drawer in her desk. At the end of each day, she would ask Jeff if he made any cold calls that day and, if so, how many.

For each call Jeff made, his assistant would remove one ten-dollar bill from the envelope and give it to him. Finally, every Friday afternoon at four o'clock, she would call Jeff to her desk and have him watch as she fed any remaining ten-dollar bills—Jeff's ten-dollar bills—to an obliging paper shredder.

So what happened? Knowing that he would have to bear the immediate pain and embarrassment of watching his hard-earned money go through the shredder, Jeff no longer had any trouble making ten cold calls a week. He still hated making the calls, but he made them anyway because he now actually felt in his gut like he had to. He had created a reason to follow through that *felt real*, *right now*—a reason that, unlike the good, logical but ineffective reason for making these calls, actually motivated him to make them.

What's important to realize is that although Jeff was convinced all along that failing to make ten cold calls a week was costing him way more than a hundred dollars a week, he didn't follow through until he created a reason that he could truly feel.

CREATING COMPELLING REASONS TO FOLLOW THROUGH

After reading *Following Through* and learning about follow-through strategies, Joe decided to use what he had learned to overcome his reluctance to go to the gym to exercise. He made a deal with himself. He agreed that from now on (1) he would restrict himself to owning only one stick of underarm deodorant, and (2) instead of keeping the deodorant in his bathroom at home, he would keep it in his locker at the gym.

That's all it took for Joe to follow through on his intention to exercise regularly. Suddenly, there was no more struggling every morning to muster enough willpower to overcome his reluctance to go to the gym. Joe now felt like he had to go to the gym—not because it was important to exercise, but because he was mortified by the idea of otherwise having to go to work or anywhere else smelling badly. So he went to the gym every day. And once he got there, he would have felt pretty foolish about just using his deodorant and then leaving, so he exercised.

And then there's James, an independent insurance agent and another reader of *Following Through*, who created a reason he could actually feel to follow through on his failing intention to prepare for a certification exam. James was convinced that passing the exam and getting certified in a specialty area he liked would be his ticket to more effectively marketing his services. He decided that the best way to prepare was to get up a half hour early every weekday to study. However, when his alarm went off at 6:30 each morning, he just couldn't make himself get out of bed and start studying.

"I'll start tomorrow," he would tell himself . . . day after day after day.

Frustrated by his poor follow-through, James decided to take the bull by the horns and create a reason he could actually feel. He bought an extra alarm clock, placed it in his kids' bedroom, and set it for 6:30 a.m. He then set his own alarm clock for 6:25 a.m. When his alarm clock went off, he felt as reluctant as ever to get out of bed and start studying. But now there was a big difference.

James knew that if he didn't get up and turn off the alarm clock in his kids' room, it would go off and wake up the kids, who didn't need to get up until much later. He also knew that if that happened, his wife would be furious with him. Suddenly getting up early had ceased to be just a good idea. Now he felt like he absolutely had to get up, which is what he did. And once James got out of bed, he would have felt just too

> Although a good reason is enough to *decide* to follow through, it takes a compelling reason—a reason you can feel in your gut right now—to *actually* follow through.

foolish about turning off the alarm clock and returning, so he studied.

Once again, the lesson is that there's a critical difference between *a good reason* for doing what you intend to do and a *reason you can actually feel*. Although a good reason is enough to *decide* to follow through, it takes a compelling reason—a reason you can feel in your gut right now—to *actually* follow through.

THREATEN TO VIOLATE YOUR INTENTION IN A BIG WAY

Although you may be thinking that we've already gone too far, fasten your seat belt because we're about to go even further.

How about a strategy that's based on a fascinating paradox? Given how easy it is to stray from your intentions, you might be surprised to learn that one of the most powerful follow-through strategies is to promise to deliberately violate your intentions in a big way if you don't do what you intend to do.

Levinson and Greider described how they used this strategy to help a woman resist the temptation to eat lots of donuts at work. They asked her only to agree that if she gave in to the temptation to eat a donut, she would have to take and eat three donuts. Although she often ate more than three donuts a day on her own, there was no way she could eat three at once *on purpose*, so she followed through on her intention and ate none.

Steve used this strategy himself to keep working on an unpleasant project that he intended to finish but kept avoiding. He simply made a deal with himself that whenever he would find himself avoiding working on the project, he'd stand up in his office with his hands in his pockets and do absolutely nothing until he was ready to sit down and get to work. He still didn't feel like working on the project, but because he felt even less like standing up like a fool and making a point of doing nothing in a big showy way, he kept his nose to the grindstone until the project was done.

Steve's client Daniel was getting disgusted with himself for repeatedly putting off working on an unappealing but important project that he intended to finish. Instead of asking him to promise to work on the project, Steve asked him to promise *not* to work on it tomorrow or the next day *unless* he worked on it today.

Sound crazy? Well, yes, but it's actually not crazy at all. As easy as it had been for Daniel to keep putting off doing something he didn't feel like doing, once he was in a situation where putting it off meant being forced to put it off even longer, he *chose* to get to work.

Alan Stevens, who is past president of the Global Speakers Federation and founder of MediaCoach, uses what could best be described as a "do it or lose it" version of this strategy. He creates a card for each task that he intends to do later. Then he follows a rule he created himself to make his intentions more effective: He deliberately places himself in danger of losing the opportunity to act on his intentions. When he reviews his task cards, if he finds a task that he's neglected to do for more than a month, he shreds the card and forbids himself from doing the task.

CREATE A SENSE OF URGENCY

Jim Beach, an entrepreneur, teacher of entrepreneurs, and coauthor of *School for Startups*, also puts an interesting twist on the idea of deliberately using a sense of urgency to promote follow-through. He practices what could probably best be described as "procrastination-powered follow-through." By essentially forbidding himself from starting a project until there's hardly any time left, he creates a sense of urgency that gets him in gear.

What's especially interesting about Jim's approach is that he actually builds a follow-through strategy directly into his intentions. He doesn't even *intend* to start work sooner. He intends to wait until the last minute. He does this on purpose because he knows that at the last minute—and not until then—he'll feel like he has no choice, which is exactly what it takes for him to get the job done.

By the way, Jim's strategy comes with a bonus. Jim doesn't suffer the way the rest of us do when we intend to start working sooner but don't actually start until much later. By making a point of waiting until he can actually feel like he must do the thing, Jim bypasses the all-too-familiar stressful and exhausting period that typically stretches painfully from the point of "I really should do it" to the point of "Okay, now I have no choice."

Of course, there are lots of examples of inspiring others to achieve higher levels of performance not by giving them *more* time, but by giving them *less* time so that they'll feel a greater sense of urgency.

In his fascinating book, *Business Secrets of the Trappist Monks: One CEO's Quest for Meaning and Authenticity*, author, entrepreneur, and corporate executive August Turak describes a strategy that some companies use to turbocharge employee productivity. They deliberately create what Turak refers to as "goat rodeos" by announcing extremely tight last-minute deadlines that throw everyone into an energizing frenzy.

As much as you may dislike feeling like you're under pressure to do something you'd rather not do, strategically turning the pressure up rather than down is often the best way to promote follow-through.

Stephen Sutton found a way to create the ultimate sense of urgency. Actually, the *way* found Stephen. He was only nineteen years old and dying of cancer. But he had a big dream to do something for other teenagers with cancer before he died. With an acute sense of urgency pushing him hard, Stephen relentlessly used social media, fund-raising, events, and speeches to raise nearly £5 million (about $7.5 million) for the Teenage Cancer Trust.

Less than three weeks before Stephen died, he was a guest on Chris's radio show along with productivity expert Mike Pagan. Chris wondered what had enabled Stephen to be so successful. "My cancer has given me so little time and so much motivation," Stephen explained. "Most people have so much time and so little motivation!"

Needless to say, Stephen made quite an impression. He was a truly remarkable young man, who harnessed the power of his own sense of urgency to turn his last good intention into action that would benefit many others.

PUTTING IT INTO PRACTICE

1. Have you ever locked yourself in a cage, burned a bridge behind you, made a public promise, or done anything else to deliberately put yourself in a jam that you could get out of only by following through?

2. Can you think of a way to make yourself follow through by deliberately putting yourself in a jam?

3. How can you make the consequences of not following through on a particular intention *feel* real?

4. What can you do to create a greater sense of urgency about following through on an intention that you're considering adopting?

5. How might you be able to make use of the strategy of requiring yourself to violate an intention in a big way if you violate it at all?

NOTES

_____

_____

_____

_____

_____

_____

_____

_____

_____

_____

_____

_____

_____

_____

_____

_____

_____

_____

_____

_____

_____

_____

_____

_____

_____

_____

CHAPTER 8

DETOXIFY DREADED TASKS

The secret of getting ahead is getting started.

—MARK TWAIN

Usually the most effective way to get yourself to do what you intend to do is to put more power behind your good intention. But there's another way, and it's also a gentler way. This strategy works by reducing the resistance you feel to doing what you intend to do. In other words, it makes the goo less gooey.

To understand this strategy, you need to first take a fresh look at what happens when you avoid doing something you've decided you should do.

The first and most obvious result of avoidance is that whatever it is that you're avoiding doing doesn't get done. But there's a second result that's easy to overlook, and it's a paradoxical one. Avoidance prevents you from building the routine or habit that

> Avoidance prevents you from building the routine or habit that would eventually make it easier for you to do what you intend to do.

would eventually make it easier for you to do what you intend to do.

It's this second consequence of avoidance that the *Detoxify Dreaded Tasks* strategy addresses. By stripping away the toxic parts of the task that you're avoiding—the parts that make it feel worth avoiding—this strategy allows you to at least move forward with building a routine.

TIPTOE AROUND THE AVOIDANCE MONSTER

Levinson and Greider used the phrase "waking up the avoidance monster" to describe what can happen when you try to coax yourself into doing a task you don't feel like doing. Experiencing the unpleasantness can intensify your desire to avoid doing the dreaded task.

By tiptoeing around the avoidance monster, Steve's client Thomas managed to do an accounting task he didn't feel at all like doing.

Thomas had concluded that he really should be reviewing his business's financial performance once a week. Although he had promised himself many times that he'd start doing these reviews "next week," he

kept putting them off because he absolutely hated accounting.

Disgusted with himself, Thomas was ready to try something different. So he stripped away everything about these reviews that had been causing him to avoid doing them. Then he promised to do only whatever was left.

By the time Thomas had stripped away everything that had been repelling him, frankly, there wasn't much left. But here's what he promised to do: Every Thursday morning at 10 a.m., he would gather up the materials he needed to do a proper review, put them on his desk, and then sit down. That's it. If he did only that much and nothing more, he told himself, he would have fulfilled his obligation, honored his commitment, kept his promise. Of course, if he just happened to feel like going further, that would be fine.

By stripping the dreaded task of everything that had been making it worth avoiding, Thomas made it possible to move forward. He was able to establish the shell of a routine of doing weekly financial reviews. He was now at least showing up regularly for these reviews, and was ready to actually look at financial information when the spirit moved him, which sometimes it did. In fact, more often than not, after doing the minimum he'd promised to do, Thomas actually did more—sometimes a lot more.

Before long, Thomas had developed a routine of doing substantive and useful weekly financial reviews.

LOWER THE BAR TO CLEAR THE HURDLE

Steve used this same strategy to follow through on his intention to exercise every day. Although his goal was to ride his exercise bike for forty minutes every morning, the very thought of having to pedal and endure boredom for forty minutes was enough to keep him in bed.

So Steve asked himself what he would have to remove from the routine to make it doable—that is, not at all worth avoiding. In other words, what was the most he could imagine doing every day without thinking, "Oh no, not that damned bike again!" The answer turned out to be "not very much at all." He could imagine putting on his exercise clothes, sitting on the bike, and putting his feet on the pedals. No problem! But he couldn't picture himself doing any more than that without taking a chance of waking up the Avoidance Monster. So he promised to do only that much (actually, that little!).

Steve kept his promise every day. It was easy. There was nothing to dread and nothing worth avoiding. What's more, once he fulfilled his obligation to put on his exercise clothes, sit on the bike, and put his feet on the pedals, he usually found himself pedaling. Sometimes he pedaled for just a few minutes. Sometimes he pedaled for a lot longer. Soon, he was pedaling for forty minutes every day. Before long, he had created a self-sustaining habit that's lasted for years.

GET THE BALL ROLLING

Steve's client Amy got the ball rolling on her office organization project.

For weeks, every time Amy thought about getting started, she woke up the Avoidance Monster. She felt a big "Oh no, not that!" in the pit of her stomach that kept her from moving forward. Scolding herself only made matters worse, and so did giving herself pep talks about how good she would feel if she finally did get the job done.

Amy dreaded organizing because she knew it would be a big and overwhelming task that would force her to make a bunch of little decisions she didn't feel at all like making. She tentatively concluded that if all she had to do was spend a minute or two a day organizing, with absolutely no expectation of accom-

THE POWER TO GET THINGS DONE

plishing anything, she wouldn't avoid doing it. So that's what she agreed to do—not one iota more.

That changed everything. Once Amy had removed all the toxins from organizing, she no longer dreaded doing it. She not only organized every day, she almost always spent much longer than a minute or two. A few times, she got on a roll and spent hours organizing.

What especially impressed Amy was that as her organizing started to produce tangible benefits, she sometimes even looked forward to spending time organizing.

COMMIT ONLY TO DOING THE EASY PART

Kathy Tracey, who we mentioned earlier, often relies on this strategy to follow through on her intention to keep herself fit.

"I break down the actions I need to take, and I commit to doing the first part of it only," she told us. "So, for example, if I should go out for a training run after a long day at work but I feel tired, I commit to putting on my running kit and shoes but not to the run."

Kathy, who is also managing director of The Learning Company Ltd., uses this same strategy whenever she faces an avoidance-worthy task at work. "I just commit to the first part. Breaking it down like this makes it all seem much more manageable," she explained. "And once you gain some momentum on a task, it's easier to keep going."

Kathy also told us about a friend who uses a similar strategy to follow through on his intention to cook proper meals for himself, which is something he often doesn't feel like doing. He promises only to cut up an onion. "And then the rest starts to happen!" Kathy explained.

Remember, the key to getting good results with this strategy is to never set any requirements as to how much you must actually accomplish beyond a simple initial step. If you start to insist on doing more than you feel like doing, you'll wake up the Avoidance Monster, and it will all be over.

This strategy is especially well suited to tasks that require creative effort.

If you've ever tried, you know how hard it can be to force creativity. In fact, too heavy-handed an approach can backfire. That's why Steve typically uses this strategy to stay on track with his writing.

> If you start to insist on doing more than you feel like doing, you'll wake up the Avoidance Monster, and it will all be over.

When he has a writing project to work on, Steve requires himself only to sit down at his computer, open the file or files he needs, close any other files, and remove any other obvious distractions. Once he sets the stage for creative work, he's done. That's right, he's done.

If the creative spirit happens to show up, great!

Steve works for as long as he feels like working. But if his muse is a no-show, which happens sometimes, he doesn't force himself to write. He doesn't struggle. He doesn't fight. He doesn't threaten. He doesn't pressure. He just leaves without creating a fuss, and he comes back later. The last thing he wants to do is make writing feel avoidance-worthy.

Using this strategy is a bit like attracting birds you'd like to watch. Your job is to simply create the most inviting conditions. The rest is up to the birds— or your muse.

A SPECIAL STRATEGY FOR DETOXIFYING STUPID TASKS

If you're an employee with a pile of *stupid goo* on your work plate, there's a special strategy that might be worth a try. Remember, stupid goo represents employer-required actions, tasks, and projects that are especially toxic because you perceive them as being wasteful, unnecessary, unreasonable, unfair, or just plain stupid. As we pointed out earlier, you're likely to feel way more resistance to, for example, filling out a form that you perceive as stupid than to filling out one you don't perceive that way.

Here's how to use this strategy:

1. Rant and rave about just how idiotic, dumb, unnecessary, unfair, and unjust the avoidance-worthy task is.

2. Repeat the step above as many times as it takes for the ranting and raving to start to feel like a chore.

3. Now take a clear look at what the task actually requires. You'll notice that the task is no longer as toxic as it seemed.

4. Do the task quickly before the *poison* returns!

PUTTING IT INTO PRACTICE

1. What are some tasks or projects you dread that could be detoxified so you can at least get started?

2. What are the nontoxic parts of these tasks or projects—the parts you wouldn't avoid?

NOTES

_____

_____

_____

_____

_____

_____

_____

_____

_____

CHAPTER 9

BUY FOLLOW-THROUGH HELP

If you chase two rabbits, both will escape.

—CHINESE PROVERB

You may not be able to buy love, but you can buy follow-through. And frankly, it can be a lot cheaper to pay for follow-through than to pay for *not* following through!

It may not be your first choice, but never rule out the possibility of reducing the amount of willpower it takes to do something you intend to do by simply paying someone else to do it for you.

Martin Palethorpe, founder of the Pragma Group, has a deep-rooted passion for advising, challenging, and inspiring leaders to develop themselves and their organizations to maximize long-term performance. His accomplishments are truly inspiring, and so is his mastery of a simple strategy that's contributed generously to his success.

> Never rule out the possibility of reducing the amount of willpower it takes to do something you intend to do by simply paying someone else to do it for you.

"I outsource everything that I am no good at," Martin explained. "I always get someone else to do it for me."

Even if you're good at something, if you're unlikely to be good at following through on it, consider delegating it to someone else who will follow through.

Obviously you can't delegate everything you're not following through on. There are some things that only you can do. There are other things that you certainly could delegate in theory, but you simply don't have the resources to make it feasible. But whenever the delegation option is available to you, there are two reasons why you should seriously consider exercising it.

The first reason is obvious. If you delegate the task to someone who, unlike you, truly must do it, the task will get done.

The second reason is less obvious but just as important. By delegating tasks or projects that you intend to do but are at risk of not doing, you prevent yourself from suffering follow-through failures. That's important because follow-through failures can reduce the effectiveness of all your intentions. When you delegate, you're demonstrating that you're taking your intentions seriously, and that can help to keep all your intentions effective.

PAY SOMEONE TO KICK YOUR BUTT

When you're the only one who can do something that must be done, you can always pay someone to see to it that you'll actually do it. This may at first sound foolish, wasteful, and unnecessary, but just think about it.

If you're not doing something that you've decided you should do, how much would it be worth to get yourself in gear? Put differently, how much will it cost you to *not* do what you intend to do? If not following through will cost you more than it would cost to hire someone to *make* you follow through, wouldn't it make sense to spend the money?

Jim Leighton, president of Perdue Foods and author of *Getting F.I.T.*, used this strategy to make sure he'd finish writing his book despite the many other demands competing for his time and attention. With a large company to run, Jim's plate was already pretty full when he decided to write a book about creating fully integrated teams. So, to make sure that he would finish, he hired experts who would not only give him guidance but would keep him focused on the book until it was done.

SOMETIMES YOU CAN GET FOLLOW-THROUGH HELP FOR FREE

Whenever you're considering the feasibility of purchasing certain business services, it's wise to consider the hidden follow-through benefits that may come along with those services. Sometimes the value of the follow-through help you can get may be much greater than the value of the service itself.

Chris marvels at how hiring a cleaner to regularly clean his home has actually caused him and his wife to do a better job of tidying their house themselves. Often when Chris and Ruth remember on Thursday evening that the cleaner will be coming on Friday, they get into a productive frenzy and tidy up the house. So for the price of the cleaning service, they are also getting help following through on their intention to keep things tidier.

If you purchase accounting services, might you also be getting valuable *accountability* services? If the services you purchase or the person or persons you hire make you feel like you must follow through on your intention to more closely monitor your business's financial performance, they can be worth their weight in gold.

If you hire a consultant who can give you sage advice about a business strategy, might the consultant also make you feel accountable for doing the hard work that will be required to break into a new market you've identified? If the answer is yes, the follow-through benefits you'll get from hiring the consultant may well exceed the value of the business advice you're paying for.

JOIN A GROUP

Steve Robinson of Si Consulting Limited (UK) joined Chris's Elevation Program to get practical business advice and training. What he ended up getting, however, was far more valuable than that. He got help following through. How? Being a member of a group of entrepreneurs who openly shared their hopes, dreams, and intentions made Steve *feel accountable* to his fellow entrepreneurs for actually doing what he intended to do.

Lots of businesspeople these days join networking or *mastermind* groups. These groups range from the informal and free to the more structured and paid for. Examples of the latter include Business Network International's Business Breakfasts and Chris's Elevation Program.

It's a wonderful concept: Like-minded businesspeople coming together to learn from each other, support each other, and sometimes collaborate. And belonging to one of these groups can bring significant follow-through benefits. The key, however, is to choose a group that emphasizes *accountability*. It may feel good to get unconditional support, but unconditional support probably won't help you follow through. If it's follow-through help you're seeking, make sure you

> It may feel good to get unconditional support, but unconditional support probably won't help you follow through.

choose a group that will make you feel obligated to do the things you say you're going to do.

HIRE A MENTOR OR COACH

Chris has gained a lot from the mentors and coaches he's worked with. However, what he's learned about following through has had quite an impact on how he works with them.

For example, Chris no longer wants to work with a coach or mentor who will let him off the hook. (He can do that perfectly well himself, thank you!) He now makes it clear that an important part of the coaching or mentoring job is to hold him accountable for doing whatever he agrees he will do to build his business. If necessary, he expects to be pushed, prodded, pestered, and even guilted into acting in accord with his intentions. If he fails to do what he agrees he will do, he expects his coach or mentor to kick his butt!

Chris insists on being held accountable for submitting detailed monthly reports to his mentor, who he perceives as a highly valued board member. Along with the usual business metrics, goals, and objectives, Chris includes something that doesn't typically show up in a business report: his intentions!

"GET THAT SPREADSHEET DONE!"

The strategy of paying people to make sure he'll follow through is certainly paying off for Chris. It's had a huge impact on his ability to turn his good intentions into action, and that in turn has had a huge impact on his business.

Within the first month of his latest financial year, he booked more consulting work than he had in any twelve-month period in the first five years of his business! Thanks to being, as Steve puts it, "willingly forced" to do whatever needs to be done, Chris has earned a tremendous return on his investment and now owns a business that he can be very proud of. And as a bonus, he no longer has to put more and more time into his business, because he's now able to put more and more business into his time!

BUY A GADGET

Okay, this may not be the most significant application of the *Buy Follow-Through* strategy, but don't overlook it. If there's an appealing gadget out there that will satisfy your inner child while helping you follow through, buying it might actually be the *adult* thing to do.

For example, have you been secretly craving one of those nifty label makers because it seems like it would just be fun to print professional-looking labels for just about everything in your office? If so, it could be worth giving in to the temptation because your new *toy* might actually help you act on your good intention to organize your office. It doesn't matter that you're more motivated to play than to get organized.

Chris recently benefited from this strategy when he bought a fine high-capacity paper shredder. He realized that wanting this shredder had a lot more to do with his childish instincts than his business instincts, but so what? Because he absolutely loves shredding with this machine, he's following through on his intention to get rid of paper clutter.

PUTTING IT INTO PRACTICE

1. Is there any follow-through help you need that you can buy?

2. Are there any groups you can join that would make you feel accountable for following through?

NOTES

PART FOUR

How to Keep On Keeping On

> People often say that motivation doesn't last. Well, neither does bathing—that's why we recommend it daily.
>
> —ZIG ZIGLAR

———————————————————

In this section, we'll show you what it takes to keep your follow-through habits strong.

CHAPTER 10

KEYS TO MAINTAINING FOLLOW-THROUGH MASTERY

Success is a ladder you cannot climb
with your hands in your pockets.

—AMERICAN PROVERB

The first key to keeping your follow-through ability strong is to make a habit of creating a follow-through plan for every good intention you adopt.

Every good intention deserves its own follow-through plan. A follow-through plan lays out *what specifically you're going to do to make sure that you'll act on a particular intention*.

You may be questioning whether you really need to develop a follow-through

> Every good intention deserves its own follow-through plan.

plan for each and every good intention you adopt. You don't. Just like you don't need a parachute each and every time you jump out of an airplane!

"Who needs a parachute?"

Okay, perhaps we're exaggerating just a bit. But developing a follow-through plan is at least as necessary as setting your alarm clock to make sure that you'll wake up at a given time. A follow-through plan is what makes the difference between, on the one hand, just crossing your fingers and hoping for the best and, on the other hand, using a deliberate, manual process to turn a good intention into action.

Developing a follow-through plan doesn't have to be a big deal. The best way to do it is by asking yourself a series of questions. The questions should make you think about the particular obstacles your good intention will face and the measures you can take to overcome those obstacles.

Once you've had some experience, you'll be able

to come up with questions that work best for you. But to get you started, here are some examples:

- What would prevent you from acting on this particular good intention?
- Will you be aware enough of your intention (or an important reason to do what you intend to do)? If there's a chance that you won't and that your good intention could get lost in the shuffle, what steps can you take to keep it on the front burner of your mind? How can you make sure that you'll be exposed to enough of the right reminders?
- What can you do to make it harder to violate your intention?
- Is there anything you can do to make it easier to do what you intend to do?
- How can you make it *feel necessary* to do what you intend to do—make it feel like you absolutely *must* do it? Can you create a situation that will essentially *force* you to follow through—that is, leave you with no choice?
- Is there anything more you can do to eliminate or at least minimize the need to rely on your willpower?

Each answer you give may well prompt other questions. Remember, what you're trying to do is identify obstacles and determine the best way to overcome them. The end result of the self-interview you conduct will be a specific measure or measures that you've decided to take to follow through on this particular intention.

To give you a better idea of how this process works, let's look at how Chris developed a follow-through plan to support his intention to combine his two websites into one. We'll start at the point where his good intention was born.

Chris had thought for some time about integrating his two websites into one. He could see lots of benefits and, other than the time, effort, and money required, no disadvantages. The benefits included having a site that he would be really proud of that would be a showcase for his new brand; a potential increase in sales revenue that would result from prospective clients appreciating the site and thinking "I must hire Chris Cooper!"; an increase in online sales; and last but not least, he could get new business cards! (Chris admits it. He loves business cards!) He realized that if he put off the project, he'd not only delay enjoying these benefits, he'd have to endure the unpleasant feeling that his website didn't do justice to the great work his business was doing.

After *wobbling* for a while, Chris decided that, all things considered, he should go for it. He made his promise: "*I will* integrate my two websites into one by the end of October." Now he was ready to start *walking*. But he had already learned the hard way that he couldn't *walk* very far without *legs,* so he went ahead and developed a follow-through plan to make sure that he'd turn his new intention into success-producing action.

First, Chris asked himself what could prevent him from following through. The answer was pretty obvious, although, he confessed, his enthusiasm had initially prevented him from seeing it clearly. He was already way too busy! His day-to-day work responsibilities, including serving clients and carrying out essential business-development activities, would make it really tough for him to deliver on something new that, unlike many of his responsibilities, didn't absolutely have to be done.

Then Chris asked himself whether he would have to take steps to keep this particular intention on the front burner of his mind. Of course he would! With so many pressing demands competing for his attention, this one wouldn't have a chance. So he thought about creating some reminders. He could put his new intention on the whiteboard he checks and updates every day. He could use his MotivAider to remind himself frequently why it was so important to complete the website project. He could include the project as a top priority in his monthly board report.

As Chris thought about involving the board, it occurred to him that putting his promise out there for the board to see would do a lot more than just help him stay aware of his good intention. It would create some *friendly pressure* that would make it much harder for him to not follow through. Perfect!

When he asked himself if there was any way to make it easier to follow through and to have to rely less on his willpower, the answer jumped out at him. Why not hire someone to manage the project? Not only would that person do some of the technical work he really didn't have time to do anyway, he or she would have to pester Chris for information, and that would keep him engaged in the project and moving forward. If all it would take to follow through was responding to questions and demands issued by someone he'd decided to pay to get the job done right and on time, Chris would surely follow through.

It was settled. He had his plan. He had measures in place to remind him of his intention so it wouldn't get lost in the shuffle, to make it hard to not follow through, to make it feel necessary to do what he intended to do, and to make it easier to do it, too. His intention now had legs. Now Chris was truly ready to *walk*.

With experience, you'll get better at cutting to the chase, and the whole process won't take you more than a few minutes to complete. Given that a follow-through plan can make the difference between following through and not, developing one for every new intention is an awfully smart investment.

ACTIVELY MANAGE YOUR INTENTION PORTFOLIO

We assume you keep track of your money and your valuables. Well, guess what? Your intentions are valuables, too. After all, they represent everything you know you should do to be as successful as possible.

So how can you keep track of your intentions? How will you know what promises you've made and whether or not you're keeping them? It matters because unless you stay on top of your promises, you'll rob them all of credibility, clout, and effectiveness.

Exactly how you keep track of your promises is up to you.

- Beverly writes each of her work-related intentions on an index card and keeps the deck of cards on her desk.
- Lewis writes each intention on a slip of paper and keeps all the slips in a large glass jar.
- Jacob keeps a list of intentions on his computer in a simple word processing file he calls "MYPROMISES."
- Chris uses a dedicated whiteboard to display his business-related intentions and his progress in implementing them.

If you're tempted to create an elaborate spreadsheet or database to keep track of your intentions, we urge you to resist the temptation. You're far better off with an extremely simple and basic system that you'll actually use than with an elaborate and sophisticated one that you'll soon abandon. So please, go easy on the bells and whistles. What matters most is that you come up with an approach that doesn't discourage you from using it.

Once you've designed a workable system for keeping track of your intentions, you're ready to schedule regular—say, weekly—*Intention Reviews*. If you're thinking, "Yeah right, like I've got time for another meeting," don't worry. These meetings can be very brief. Seriously, even if you set aside as little as five or ten minutes a week to devote your undivided attention to your list of intentions, we're confident that you'll be rewarded by an improvement in follow-through.

So how do you conduct an Intention Review? It's easy. You simply ask yourself questions like these:

- How am I doing at following through in general? Am I mostly making the right promises? Am I mostly keeping them?
- Have I stated my intentions clearly enough to eliminate wiggle room and make myself feel properly accountable for doing what I intend to do?
- Are there any intentions I should cross off my list because they're no longer necessary; they conflict with other intentions that I've decided are more important; they're unrealistic; or there's no way I'm going to follow through on them anyway?
- Do I have a follow-through strategy or strategies in place for each intention?
- Are there any intentions that call for a change in strategy?

- Do I have room to take on more intentions, or am I already maxed out?

We'll let you in on a secret. How you answer these questions isn't that important. What matters most is that you keep asking them. Their main purpose is to force you to be explicit about how you deal with your intentions so that you'll never again slip back into taking a hands-off approach that allows you to put them off.

Can you go further than this to stay on top of your intentions? Of course you can. If you do, just make sure that you have a strategy in place to make sure that—you guessed it—you'll follow through.

"My portfolio of good intentions
is a lot bigger than my portfolio
of completed work."

GET RID OF OUTDATED INTENTIONS

Things change. Sometimes a perfectly good promise you've made just doesn't make sense anymore. Maybe your priorities have changed. Maybe your circumstances have changed. Maybe you've determined that the benefits of behaving in accord with a particular promise no longer justify the *costs*. For whatever reason, there you are with a good intention in your portfolio that no longer seems as *good* as it did when you adopted it.

What should you do?

Well, the worst thing you can do is leave a promise on the books if you're no longer fully committed to keeping it. If you just ignore it, you run the risk of reducing the credibility and clout of all your promises. The best way to handle a promise that's no longer valid is to *formally* remove it from your portfolio. Notice that we made a point of saying *formally*. That's because you need to have a ceremony of sorts whenever you remove an intention. After all, you're doing something a little tricky. You're trying to get rid of an intention that's no longer valid without also diminishing the value of all your other intentions, present and future. So you need to be very explicit about announcing to yourself that you're removing a particular intention from your portfolio because you've made an intelligent decision to do so—not because you simply failed to follow through—and that you're no longer holding yourself accountable for acting on this particular intention.

> Being exquisitely explicit about how you handle your intentions is a key to keeping them effective.

We realize that it may

seem silly to make such a big production out of removing an intention from your portfolio, but being exquisitely explicit about how you handle your intentions is a key to keeping them effective.

AIM FOR NO UNKEPT PROMISES

Improving your follow-through ability is not just a way to be productive. It's also a way to achieve contentment and personal satisfaction that goes well beyond success.

But contentment and personal satisfaction don't come simply from keeping lots of promises. They come from keeping all the promises you make—from leaving no promises unkept. That means that your inclination to make promises must be *in sync* with your ability to keep promises. Steve had a consulting experience years ago with a company that was having problems because a group of employees who made promises to customers wasn't on the same wavelength as a group of employees who had to keep those promises. The company's promise-makers were making promises that the promise-keepers simply couldn't keep.

Things were clearly out of balance. As a result, employee stress and conflict were high, and morale and performance were declining. To achieve balance, the promise-makers had to adjust their promising to match the realistic capacity of the promise-keepers.

Having unkept promises is like being in debt. To avoid debt and enjoy the peace of mind that comes from being debt-free, you have to keep your spending in sync with your income. If you're spending more than you're earning, you have to make some adjustments to get things back in balance. If you can't earn more, you just have to spend less.

To enjoy contentment and personal satisfaction beyond success, you have to be *promise debt-free*. So, even if you're keeping lots of promises, if you're also leaving lots of promises unkept, it's time to make some adjustments. If you can, improve your follow-through ability. But if you can't, by all means, cut back on your promise-making.

Remember, if it's contentment and personal satisfaction that you're after, it's better to make fewer promises and keep them all than it is to make more promises that you can't keep.

DON'T REST ON YOUR LAURELS

Once, while waiting in an optometrist's office, Steve watched a technician put a pair of newly fashioned eyeglasses on a patient's face. The patient gazed through his pristine new prescription lenses and smiled a great big smile. He was obviously delighted with how much better he could see.

"Wow, I can see so clearly now," he exclaimed, "I don't think I need glasses anymore!"

The man was only kidding. He knew that he was suddenly able to see so well only *because* he was wearing new, squeaky-clean glasses. But there was a keen insight embedded in his joke: When we're performing well, we don't always notice the *props* that are making it possible for us to perform well.

What does this have to do with following through? A lot, really. Once you start doing a much better job of doing what you intend to do because you're using the tools you've learned in this book, you may be tempted to stop using the tools because "I'm doing so much better now, thank you."

Unfortunately, we're not just idly speculating about what might happen. We've seen it happen. People learn how to follow through, and they use what they've learned to get fantastic results. They thoroughly enjoy their follow-through successes. But after a while, they get cocky and careless. Thinking that their follow-through problems have somehow been permanently solved, they stop deliberately taking measures to make sure that they'll do what they intend to do. Before long, they're back to square one.

Yes, there's a good chance that you'll be tempted at some point to go back to just relying on your good intentions to implement themselves. Please, please, please don't do it!

> You'll have to follow through deliberately and manually forever

If you're serious about doing what you intend to do, you'll have to follow through deliberately and manually forever.

With practice and experience, will you get better at doing it deliberately and manually? Yes, absolutely. But will you ever get to the point where doing whatever you intend to do becomes entirely natural and automatic? Probably not.

NEVER TAKE FOLLOWING THROUGH FOR GRANTED

Chris has learned not to be fooled by his follow-through successes. Although he's proud of a follow-through record that's improved by leaps and bounds, he never takes following through for granted. He knows that a key to lasting success is to never ever stop being explicit, deliberate, and strategic about how he treats his own intentions.

That's why when Chris decided that it was finally time to make good on his childhood dream of becoming a great rock guitar player, he didn't count on his excitement or even his impressive record of recent follow-through successes to make his dream come true.

Chris bought himself a beautiful Paul Reed Smith guitar and a Marshall amp, but he didn't stop there. This time, instead of just assuming that he'd follow through, which is what he had done several times before, he made a point of setting aside other pursuits, such as running marathons, playing golf, and doing anything else that would likely interfere with his guitar-playing. Then he made a point of committing to play with musicians, like his neighbor, Peter, a great drummer who Chris knew would make him feel accountable for learning, practicing, and mastering new material. And he deliberately went way out on a limb by promising people he didn't dare disappoint that within five years he would be able to perform professionally in front of a live audience. Of course, he also made a point of creating a path made up of smaller promises that kept him moving in the direction of keeping that big promise. He promised, for example, to play for friends in his garden and to play at a speaking event.

By applying the principles in this book, Chris was able to make his childhood dream come true. Today, Chris is an accomplished rock guitarist. And he's even found a way to incorporate his guitar playing into his role as a professional speaker.

And speaking of speaking, Chris also used his follow-through skills to make good on his intention to become a fine keynote speaker.

After gobbling up all the training he could get, Chris made a point of joining speakers' organizations, taking on mentors, and generally doing everything he could possibly do to associate with people and situations that he believed would make him feel accountable for following through. And he made a point of pulling the "I will" lever whenever he encountered an opportunity to speak or to do anything else that would reinforce his identity as a speaker.

Chris deliberately crawled out on limb after limb after limb to force himself to do what he intended to do. His finest moment was when Deri Llewellyn-Davies, owner and founder of Business Growth International and author of *BGI Strategy on a Page*, invited Chris to speak at the Business Growth International Super Congress in London.

Deri asked Chris to give a keynote speech on *Accountability*. The topic, of course, was perfect! But he was petrified when he learned that if he accepted, he'd be sharing the podium with several of the top speakers in the United Kingdom. These were personal heroes of his—true giants in the speaking field—and he felt he was way out of his league. Yikes! To make matters worse, Chris had never before given a speech on accountability, and he realized that preparing one would require an enormous amount of time and effort.

Chris wanted rather badly to decline the invitation. In fact, he probably would have declined if it weren't for the fact that Deri, who, after sensing Chris's hesitation, said, "If you don't want to do it, I completely understand. However, another option is that I and the event hold you accountable for producing a great keynote on accountability!"

Chris was trapped! There was no way he could turn down the invitation without being guilty of failing to practice what he preaches. So he accepted. And in doing so, he knowingly put himself in one of the biggest—and most productive—jams he had ever been in.

Just a few short months later, Chris was on the stage shoulder-to-shoulder with his heroes. He was now in their league. With the video cameras rolling, he engaged, entertained, and enlightened a pleasantly surprised audience. After his speech, he posed for photos and fielded inquiries about his availability for other major speaking engagements. Chris had made good on his dream of becoming a professional keynote speaker.

He eventually became a regional president of the Professional Speaking Association (UK), which meant that everyone expected him to be a great speaker. That kept Chris on his toes, which is exactly where he wanted to be.

Chris helps his clients stay on their toes, too. He makes accountability a critical part of the one-on-one mentoring and coaching he does.

IT'S UP TO YOU

Perhaps you've heard the story about a man who had reached the end of his rope. He was on the verge of being unable to afford food and shelter. Feeling desperate, he got down on his knees and started to pray.

"Dear God, I beg you, could you please let me win the lottery?"

Suddenly a booming voice answered from the heavens.

"Okay, I'll let you win," God said. "But you'll have to buy your own lottery ticket!"

We believe we've given you a set of powerful tools. If you use them, you can follow through like a champion and position yourself for greater success. But it's up to you to use these tools. It's up to you to follow through on following through!

If you now agree with each of the statements below, congratulations! You've accomplished a great

deal. You've made a potentially life-changing transition from trying harder to get things done to trying smarter. You're ready to begin enjoying the benefits of being able to do whatever you intend to do.

✓ My ability to follow through is vital to my success.

✓ My intentions can be effective only if I take them seriously.

✓ Although I'm motivated to be successful, I can't count on that motivation to make me do the unappealing things I know I must do to be successful.

✓ I must make a practice of taking deliberate action to encourage, pressure, trick, or even force myself to do whatever I intend to do.

✓ I won't rely on willpower unless it's absolutely necessary.

✓ With practice, I can get better and better at following through manually, but I can never ever count on automatically doing what I intend to do. I must always be deliberate, strategic, and creative about getting myself to do whatever I intend to do.

We wish you much success in turning your intentions—large and small, present and future—into tangible results that contribute generously to your success.

PUTTING IT INTO PRACTICE

1. Take one of your good intentions and develop a simple follow-through plan for it. Now do the same from now on whenever you adopt an intention.

2. What ideas do you have for a simple system that will allow you to stay on top of your good intentions? Okay, can you make it even simpler?

3. Are your promise-making and promise-keeping in sync? If not, what can you do, and what will you do, to balance them?

4. Can you imagine being fooled by your follow-through successes into thinking that you're "cured" and don't need to make a big deal of following through anymore? If so, write this ten times below: "I realize and accept that I will have to follow through deliberately and manually forever!" (Just kidding.)

5. Congratulate yourself for taking the time to learn what it really takes to turn your good intentions into success-producing action.

NOTES

_____
_____
_____
_____
_____
_____
_____
_____
_____
_____
_____
_____
_____
_____
_____
_____
_____
_____
_____
_____
_____
_____
_____
_____
_____
_____
_____
_____

ACKNOWLEDGMENTS

First, we'd like to thank Marian Lizzi, editor in chief of Perigee Books, an imprint of Penguin Random House, and our literary agent, Jeff Herman of the Jeff Herman Agency. We're grateful for the confidence that Marian and Jeff placed in us and for the outstanding guidance they provided throughout this project.

A special thanks to Huw Aaron, who created all the cartoons for this book. We were drawn to Huw by his humor, artistic talent, and style. We didn't realize that we'd also be getting a wonderful collaborator who truly understood our objectives and was eager to help us achieve them.

Steve: I'd like to thank my wife, Teresa, my sounding board in chief, for the countless hours of feedback and editorial assistance she contributed to this project. I would have been grateful had she merely tolerated my obsession, but she did way more than that. She jumped in with both feet and helped immensely. Thanks also to my amazing daughter, Kate. Whenever I needed an extra shot of motivation, all I had to do was imagine her feeling half as proud of me as I am of her. It worked every time!

Chris: I'd like to thank my wife, Ruth, for her love and support, which included giving up a family holiday so that Steve and I could finish writing the book. Also, thanks to my children, Matthew and Daniel, who give me joy, ground me, and inspire me to want to leave an inspiring legacy; and to my parents for bringing me up well. Thanks to my friends at the Professional Speaking Association and Voice America, and to Helen Urwin, Doug D'Aubrey, and Peter Roper for helping me play a bigger game.

Steve and Chris: We'd like to thank the many people on both sides of the Atlantic who contributed valuable encouragement, input, and feedback. Special thanks go to Tim Benedict, Chris Crouch, Lyle Hanson, Ian Hudson, Catherine Johnson, Andy Lopata, Darla McWilliam, and Dr. John Tyler.

Finally, we'd like to thank each other. With an ocean between us, language and cultural differences to contend with, and different career paths that brought us both to the same topic from very different angles, collaborating wasn't always easy. But we stuck with it.

Even when we disagreed, we treated each other with respect and patience. We never deviated from our simple rule: *If it doesn't work for both of us, it doesn't go in the book.* And in the end, the obstacles we faced were no match for the passion we share for teaching people how to consistently turn their good intentions into success-producing action.

ABOUT THE AUTHORS

Teresa Levinson

Martin Neeves Photography LTD

Steve Levinson, PhD, is a clinical psychologist who draws on over four decades of varied experience as a clinician, health care executive, and innovator, teacher, consultant, inventor, and entrepreneur to help people follow through on their own good intentions.

Born and raised in New York City, Steve earned a bachelor's degree in psychology from Queen's College of the City University of New York and a PhD in clinical psychology from the University of Rochester. He moved to Minnesota in the 1970s to develop and direct an innovative rural mental health program that flourished under his leadership for thirty-five years.

Steve is recognized internationally as an expert

on the topic of following through. After developing a groundbreaking theory that explains why even highly motivated people often do a lousy job of following through on their own good intentions, he teamed up in the 1990s with peak-performance business consultant Pete Greider to write *Following Through: A Revolutionary New Model for Finishing Whatever You Start*. Levinson and Greider have been widely recognized for offering unique insights and bold solutions that enable people to consistently turn their good intentions into action.

Steve may be best known as the inventor of the MotivAider, a remarkably simple electronic device that helps users of all ages easily make desired changes in their own behavior and habits. The device, which has applications in the education, health care, business, sports, and self-improvement fields, is used in more than fifty countries.

Steve is currently president of Behavioral Dynamics Inc., a Minnesota company he cofounded in 1987 to develop, manufacture, and distribute the MotivAider and support its users worldwide. He also consults, coaches, and speaks on the topic of following through.

Steve and his wife, Teresa, live in rural Minnesota, where they enjoy wide-open spaces and uncluttered living.

Steve's website: http://habitchange.com

Chris Cooper is a business consultant, executive mentor and coach, facilitator, radio show host, and keynote speaker who is dedicated to helping the business community elevate its performance.

Born in England, Chris earned a degree in business studies and went on to work in senior roles for major companies in the United Kingdom and Australia including Rank Xerox, Mars Confectionery, United Biscuits, and Punch and Spirit Pub Groups. His various executive-level positions in sales, marketing, training, HR, procurement, and logistics enabled him to develop a very thorough understanding of business.

Chris sold his share of his first successful consultancy in 2007 to focus on his passion for business elevation. Today his services are in demand from start-ups to major brands. He hosts a widely acclaimed radio show that helps entrepreneurs and business leaders in more than fifty countries improve their skills and grow their businesses. Chris is also a popular speaker who presents at events and conferences on the topic of getting things done.

Chris has a big passion for self-development. Certified in the use of a number of business-improvement tools, he helps his clients develop the knowledge, attitude, and skills they need to achieve their business goals.

Chris lives in Leicestershire, England, with his wife, Ruth, who is a general practitioner, and his two sons, Matthew and Daniel. His favorite hobbies are playing rock guitar and fly-fishing.

Chris's website: http://chriscooper.co.uk